MENSTON
REMEMBERED

Being a look at the village, the author has lived in,
and loved, all his life, now over 90 years.

He records some changes that have taken place.
Highlighting areas of interest, some of its buildings
and institutions and meeting some of its personalities.

MENSTON REMEMBERED

Memories of a Yorkshire Village

JACK H. KELL

2014

First published in 2014 by
Croft Publications
The Croft
8 St James Meadow
Boroughbridge YO51 9NW

ISBN 978 0 9555126 9 8

Front cover illustration
from an original painting by Susan M. Ridyard

Printed and bound by
Smith Settle Printing and Bookbinding Ltd
Gateway Drive, Yeadon LS19 7XY

CONTENTS

FOREWORD

I AM honoured to be asked by Jack to write a foreword for this latest book recording the history of Menston and its characters.

Over my lifetime our friendship has grown as we shared our mutual love of Menston and its history and, in common with other Menston families, our family has benefited from one of his other loves, cricket. My wife Margaret has spent many happy hours at the cricket field watching Jack supervise, encourage and coach so many Menston youngsters.

Jack has a limitless fund of memories and anecdotes of Menston and it is only due to his skill in recording them that those who live in the village can truly appreciate their good fortune.

Menston is magical. Jack's newest book has captured its very essence as he unfolds a fascinating page by page glimpse of its history.

Dale Smith, Menston

PREFACE

Much of Menston's early history has been admirably covered by Miss Elsie Fletcher and Mr Alastair Laurence.

They have both dealt comprehensively with the beginnings of the village and its connections with the Hawksworth, Rhodes, Fairfax and Fawkes families, all of whom were closely involved in its early development. Mrs Gladys Baker did a great deal of valuable research in her popular slide lecture on Menston which she presented to most village organisations before her untimely death in 1976.

Miss Fletcher's book, *The Story of Menston* was published to coincide with the Queen's Coronation in 1952. She also regarded it as a challenge to Archdeacon Lowe of Guiseley who once told her 'Menston has no history!'.

Her 'story', which began with stone-age people, was brought up to date at the time of the Silver Jubilee, very competently, by another Menstonian, Mr Frank Voigt.

The latest investigation into Menston's history by Mr Laurence is his splendid *History of Menston and Hawksworth* published by Smith Settle in 1991. Mr Laurence having had access to the Fawkes records at Farnley Hall and the skill and tenacity of a professional historian has produced a remarkable historical record which I strongly recommend to all who love this village of ours. Milton Hudson has produced a very detailed and interesting account of nineteenth century Menston.

I do not presume to be the 'Historical Guru' of the Menston district Alastair mentions in his preface but, as a Menstonian, having seen several decades of change and development, I feel I might qualify in a small degree to be the 'One Other than Myself' Alastair also mentions.

There are occasional glimpses of the distant past 'in and amongst' but my main object is to take a closer look into modern Menston which really began say, just over 100 years ago with the coming of the Railway and the building of Highroyds Hospital or as it was originally known, Menston Asylum.

My material is largely derived from my scrapbook on Menston compiled as a labour of love over the years – and is mainly cuttings from the columns of the *Wharfedale and Airedale Observer*, which was first published in 1880.

I have also used some of Mrs Baker's unpublished notes and photographs, and other photographs have been loaned by friends.

Countless conversations with Menstonians, past and present, have produced additional valuable information and I have made some references to the works of Miss Fletcher and Mr Laurence.

ACKNOWLEDGEMENTS

A NUMBER of people have contributed to *Menston Remembered* and, apart from those mentioned in the preface, and under some photographs, I am particularly grateful to the following for their practical help and encouragement:

Margaret Brierley, Dennis Cowgill, Christine Grady, Barbara Hannam, Milton Hudson, Robert Kell, Kenneth Maston, Terry Nicholson (Croft Publications), Dr. Julian Roberts, Ken Settle, Alan Smethurst, David Stradling, Dale Smith, Peggy Turner and Margaret Wilkinson.

Also thanks to The Librarians at Ilkley Library, Jean Terry for typing the main of the manuscript and Ken Smith, formerly of Smith Settle for his early support and professional advice.

Finally, thanks to my wife, Marjorie for her patience and tolerance during the books' compilation and for frequently explaining that there are other places and people beyond the boundaries of Menston!

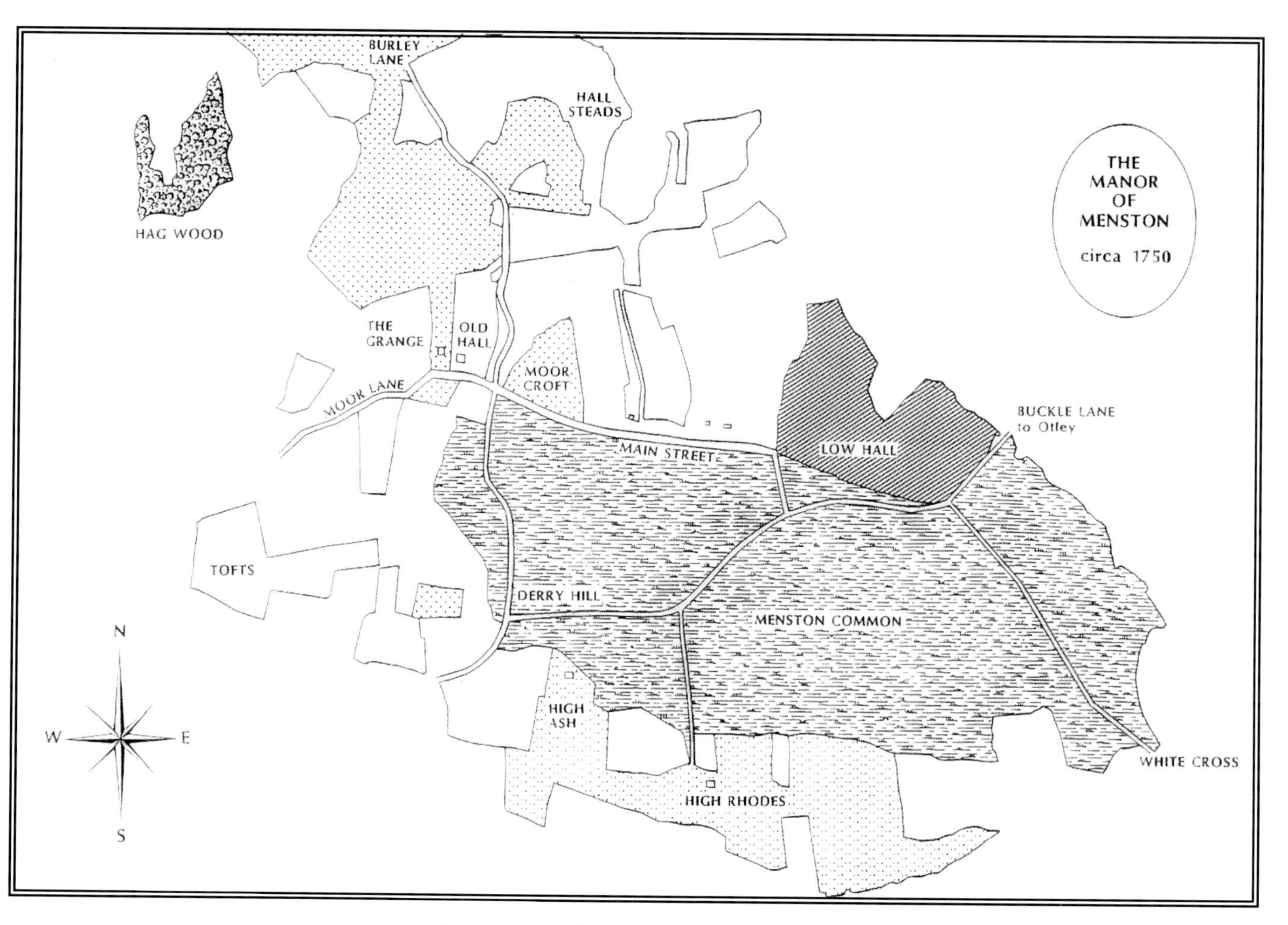

The Manor of Menston Circa 1750.

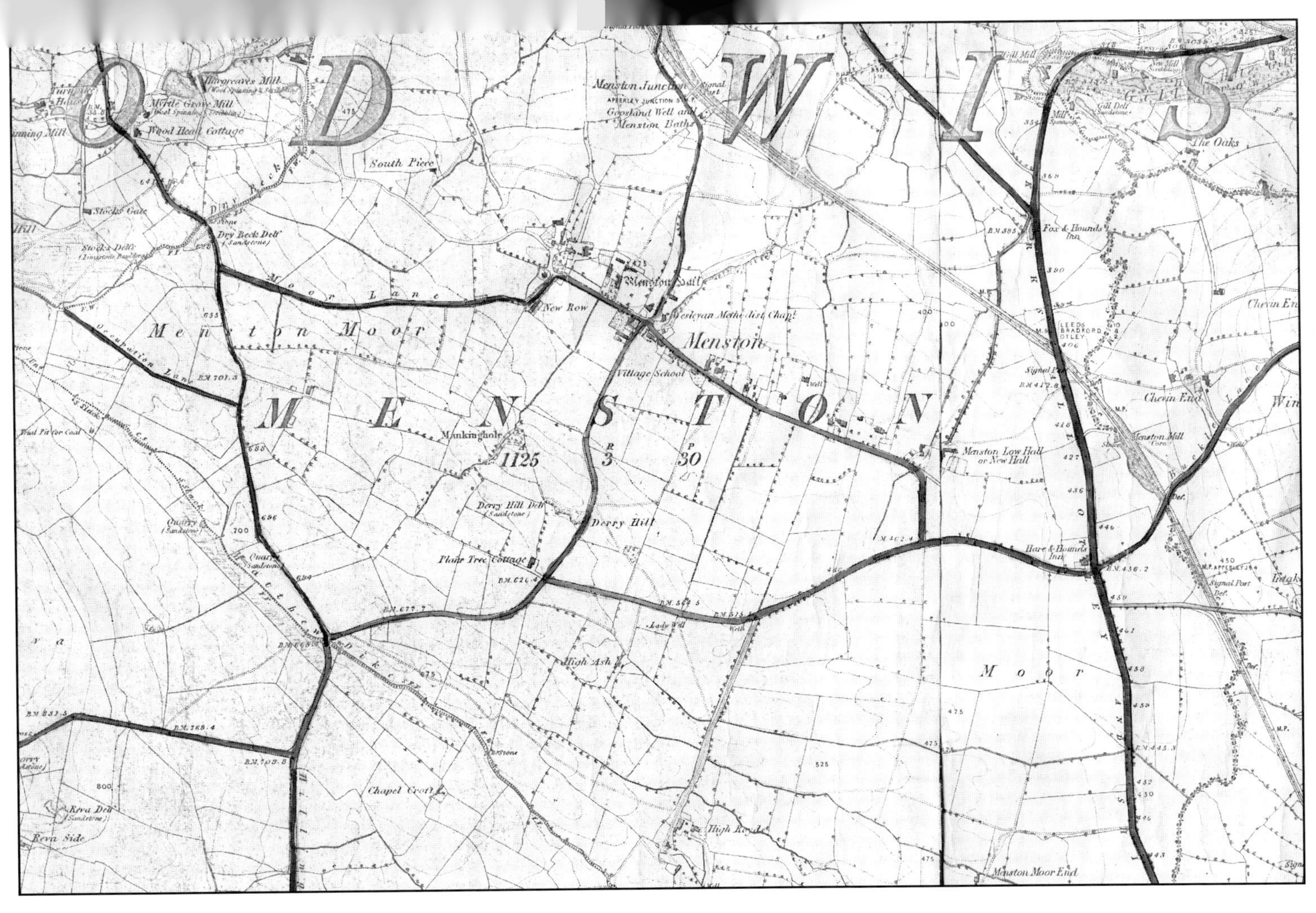

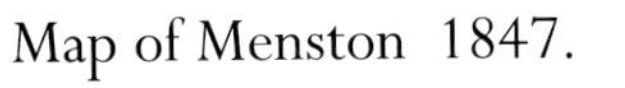
Map of Menston 1847.

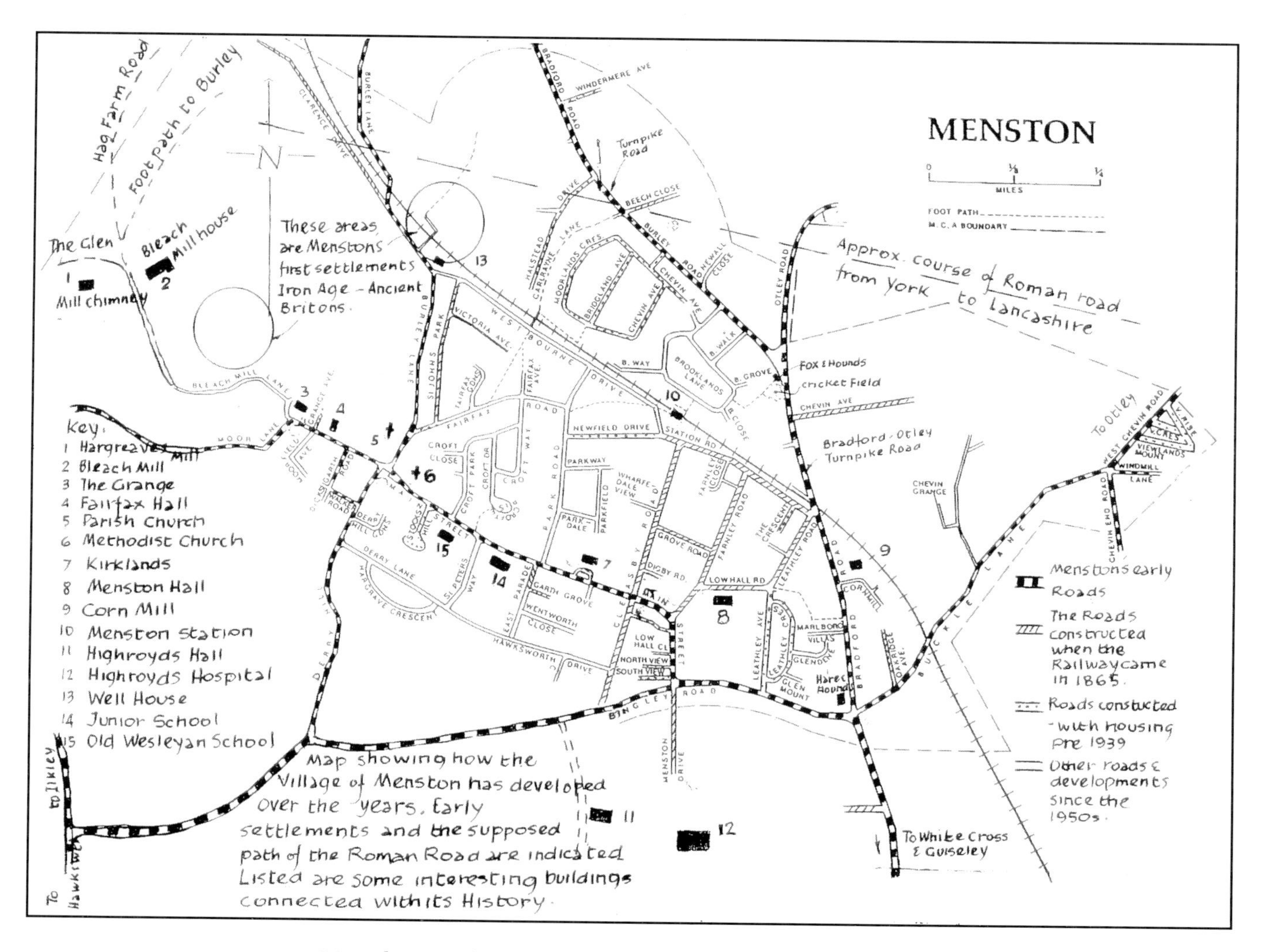

Map showing how the village has developed over the years.

EARLY ROADS AND HOUSES

About a century ago Menston was little more than a hamlet with a population of around 700 – excluding the inmates and staff of the Asylum. The population had decreased in 1871 as machine looms in the mills at Burley, Otley and Guiseley superseded the old cottage hand looms.

(Alastair Laurence records that in the middle of the nineteenth century, over 110 Menston residents worked at home producing worsted fibres.) Looking at the 1847 map there is mainly a concentration of cottage properties at Lane Ends, the two Halls, the Grange, several isolated farms and some of the stately Victorian houses on one side of Main Street.

In Cleasby Road there were only Red House, Fern Bank and the two pairs of Semis in Wharfedale View. Other houses existed in the unmade Station, Farnley and Leathley Roads. Towards the main highway were Marlborough Cottages and Marlborough Villas. Housing some of the Hospital staff were South and North Views – locally dubbed the 'Asylum Barracks'.

Expansion of the village was being encouraged by Mr Ayscough Fawkes whose family had owned the Menston Estate since 1786. He had released land on which to build the Asylum and the Railway and was now prepared to release more of the estate for houses and shops. The Midland Railway Company had elaborate plans to build a Station Hotel at the bottom of Cleasby Road.

The Wesleyans had built a new Church in 1886 to supersede the original 'square galleried box' at Lane Ends (built 1826) and the Parish Church of St. John has been open for worship since 1871. A new 'board' school, considered by some as way ahead of its time, was opened in 1894 replacing the small church schools used previously.

As the village grew, mainly due to the Asylum and easy access, by rail, to Leeds and Bradford, so did its social and sporting activities. In the late 19th century there was a lively Village Guild and frequent concerts by the Wesleyan Band of Hope, and Parish Church organisations.

In 1909, Menston St. John's Brotherhood formed 'for the social and moral welfare of its members', met twice a week and had an average attendance of forty. There was an Association Football Club and well organised Cricket, Bowling and Tennis Clubs.

In spite of these healthy indications of rapid growth however, there was much to be done in the way of services and amenities and the village came in for some severe criticism at this time. The Wharfedale and Airedale Observer took up the cause for its improvements in several scathing comments. 1881 'The principal road known as Towngate (Main Street) is in a bad state of repair, the heavy rain having carried the bed of the road away. This is all the more reprehensible when it is considered that there are drains amply sufficient to take away the flood water if the entrance to the same is adequate.'

1882 A reader asks the question:

'When will Menston people band themselves together and put a dozen street lamps in the village? Even those who are familiar with the twisting and turning characteristics of Menston's streets, by paths and lanes can only make progress by bumps and jolts at the cost of grazed shins and broken noses.'

1882 It is suggested that the centre of Menston needs improving 'There is an old combing shop which thrusts its ugly head into undue imminence in the centre of the village, may we point out that this piece of property is for sale. If the 'board' acquired it and demolished it they would affect an immense improvement to the principal thoroughfare of the village and Menston can do with improving!'

1882 A comment on behaviour: 'An appeal was made to the policeman in charge of Menston to 'move on' the roughs who congregated at street corners every Sunday night and jeered at passing Church goers.'

1883 'Menston has complained bitterly because it has not the convenience of a telegraph office. At present, with something like a thousand inhabitants they must pay a shilling for a special messenger to Otley. What with its unlighted streets, lack of telegraph facilities and muddy paths, Menston is a very benighted place indeed and does not hold many claims to the weary city toiler to come and take up his residence there!'

An observation about the village in 1890: Mrs Jane Crowther, who wrote to Miss Fletcher in 1952, recalled that, as a girl she lived with her family at Well House until 1882. 'Before St. John's Park was a lovely big field owned by Mr Willis of Burley Woodhead, one could hear corncrakes. There was no Post Office, letters were brought from Guiseley and put in old Ben Walker's shop window for people to collect. No doctor – we had Dr. Murray from Burley, a grand old gentleman who rode a white horse. No butcher's shop – a man came from Shipley on a Saturday with a nice clean cart full of meat. Ben Walker was the only grocer at Lane Ends with his wife Betty. No water in the house and only candles and oil lamps. We did have a policeman. Some lovely big houses were being built, mostly by Bradford businessmen'.

Peates of Nunroyd Guiseley wanted to buy land in Menston for their mill, but Mr Fawkes decreed that no land should be sold for industrial purposes.

Roads in the village at this time were generally extremely primitive and Walter 'Barber' Jones who came to Menston in 1898 when Carlbourne Villas were being built, described Main Street as little more than a cart track. One of my own early memories is seeing the Fison Mill Wagon – which took employees to Burley, being stuck in the mud in Stocks Hill opposite the Methodist Church.

There were always piles of loose stones kept by the Council on the south side of Main Street to fill in the pot holes. On the opposite side was a stone flagged pavement the length of the street out to the Hare and Hounds.

I remember Park Road and Leathley Avenue were green lanes. In one of his many interesting articles, my friend the late Eric Rodgers, explained the construction of highways before the advent of Tar Macadam:

Grated limestone was spread thickly to make the surface, then crushed and consolidated by a large steam roller. At the front was a great roller and at the rear were two enormously wide wheels. Behind them a number of scarifiers – sprays of water dribbled on to the roller and wheels so that the crushed stone made its own cementing slurry. The result was dry roads in summer, thick with dust, and in winter, deep in slimy, squelchy mud!'

Oakridge Avenue, Halstead Drive, Garth Grove and Grange Avenue were new developments in the thirties.

Houses on the 'Butterfield' estate were built in Bingley Road and forming the present Leathley Crescent and Avenue, (the old Green Lane). The selling price of these new properties ranged between £425 and £528.

According to Gladys Baker, after Leathley Crescent and Avenue were built, the remaining spare land towards the main road was given by Butterfields to Ilkley Urban District Council, to be used as a small playground (Incidentally, the Council sold the land in 1959 to a private builder for Glen Dene and Glen Mount.).

Houses sprang up around Chevin End and a few were built in Newfield Drive which was originally a cul-de-sac and named Harold Grove.

The Homestead estate began development, C W Bridgeland formed a consortium, mainly of building tradesmen and Fred Atkinson, assisted by William Christian (plumber) and Albert Watson (joiner), built the first five or six houses. The land was bought from Jonathan Peate and each house and garden occupied a quarter of an acre.

Stocks Hill Estate, with houses to rent, was built by the Council on land bought from my grandfather Robert Kell, by a compulsory purchase order in 1927. Building took place in odd corners of the village. Sam Oddy built a bungalow, in which to spend his retirement, at the top of Bingley Road towards Matthew Dyke, (now Sunnymeade Kennels). He, or his wife, decided that the location was too remote from the village (there were very few motor car owners at that time) so, he bought a piece of land next to Croft Cottage in Main Street and built the existing, similar, bungalow.

The greatest expansion of village housing, however, took place during the nineteen fifties and sixties. The population increased from 5331 in 1951 to 6089 in 1971. New houses filled the wide open spaces north and south of Main Street, Hawksworth Drive, Derry Lane and Wentworth Close on one side, and on the other, Croft Park, Park Road, Fairfax Road (once the 'Station fields') and Brooklands on the other. Park Road (another old Green Lane) was extended to join Westbourne Drive which was also being built upon.

St. Peter's Way (where the name came from I can't imagine) was constructed in the sixties on which was built the Infants School and Heather Court, originally as an old people's home. It was in this area that Menston's time honoured Feast was held for a few years when the Brooklands field was no longer available. Here also, at one time, Menston's St. John's played football.

Houses and flats, forming Kirklands Close and Cleasby Court, were built in 1964 on land which had been released by Mr Dick Todd of Beech House, during the war, for allotments.

After a short period as a hotel, Croft House was converted into flats in the fifties and, ten years later, Croft Court flats were added despite strong opposition from Menston's Councillors and protests from nearly 200 local residents.

Another area was developed between Low Hall Road and Farnley Road which had been Mr Cooper's orchard and where Mr Gregson, the newsagent, kept bees.

Hillside, Dr. Myer's house in Derry Hill, which had fallen into disrepair since his death in 1938, was demolished to accommodate Hillside Court – built 1981.

Since 1980 the elegant Victorian houses Elmete Grange, Willow Grove and Holly Bank, which added so much charm and character to Main Street, have all disappeared to make way for flats and modern dwellings.

Part of the Whiddon Estate, next to the Vicarage, owned in my youth by the Pearson-Cravens and later by the Sharpes, was sold, on which to build the prestigious Craven Park. Red House still stands in Cleasby Road around which are built 4 detached houses.

The same cannot be applied to West Winds in Moor Lane, a lovely house and garden designed for the late Stanley Ryley by his son Michael, less than fifty years ago. The house was summarily demolished in 1994, despite local opposition, to make way for seven houses.

Grosvenor Terrace and Carlbourne Villas c1910.

The turn of the century saw the development of St. John's Park, Grosvenor Terrace, Carlbourne Villas and Clarence Drive. The large semi-detached houses in Main Street were built by Jabez Cole and building began of Grosvenor Terrace and Carlbourne Villas, the names of which have now disappeared.

Between the Wars, with the advent of the 'modern' semi and bungalow, the large Victorian houses with their lofty rooms to be cleaned, heated and decorated, became less popular. I remember, in the thirties, houses in Carlbourne Villas being empty for months, even years, and I have learnt from Mrs Gloria Maston that her grandfather, Laurence Bell, actually bought one for £250!

The domestic servants who slept in the attics and worked long hours in the cellar kitchens were finding more congenial employment in factories and shops.

Other substantial properties were built in the new unmade Cleasby, Farnley, Station and Leathley Roads by the incoming businessmen from Leeds and Bradford.

The shops in Cleasby Road were built on land where once stood Poplar Farm. I am told they were built in thirteen weeks and each shop had some small feature of the farmhouse built into it, e.g. a window-sill or door lintel.

My earliest recollections of occupants were: Charles Land (shoe repairer), Walter Jones (hairdresser and tobacconist), Sam Wilson (newsagent), Charles Smith (plumber and ironmonger) and Sam Shelton (baker and confectioner). Incidentally, Mr Jones charged me four old pence for a hair cut!

Cleasby road – Main Street crossroads about 1930.

Beech House, from Cleasby Road where, in 1970, to the left, Hawksworth Drive was developed – below.

Two views of Bingley Road (previously Hawksworth Road) leading from the Hare and Hounds. Highroyds, or Chevin Park, on the left and now, on the right the 'Butterfields' estate – Leathley Avenue and Crescent, built in the late thirties.

Elmete Grange – demolished 1982 replaced by the flats below.

Elmete Grange

Built by Octavious Atkinson of Leeds in 1897, it had several occupants including the families of Taylor, Bains and Little before being acquired, in the nineteen twenties, by Dr. T (Tommy) G Rankine as a partner for the then ageing Dr. Hyslop.

Following Dr. Rankine in the house for a short period was Dr. McPhee. Another partner at this time was Dr. John R Gourlay, an all round sportsman, playing rugby for Otley and captain of the Menston Cricket Club when the famous Bill Bowes played after his release from a POW camp in 1945.

The Surgery, seen on the left of the house, was from where for many years, one heard the familiar voice of Barbara Lupton announce 'Doctors Purdie, Foster and Shaw' when seeking an appointment.

Dr. Foster was the last occupant before the property was demolished in 1982 for the present day flats. He retired to his native county of Gloucester in 1983, 'well respected for his bedside manner, particularly by his older patients.' He died in 1995.

Dr. David Purdie was in practice for some forty years and died, in retirement, in 1987. In a tribute which I fully endorse, he was described as 'the epitome of the family doctor, a wise, kindly and quietly efficient medical man trusted by all his patients.'

Dr. Harry Shaw was another well respected G. P. until he retired in 1984. He died in 1997 and had lived in Menston since the age of thirteen.

Dr. Shaw supported several village organisations including the annual Menston Show. His house was the one which overlooks the cricket field, on the A65, and the garden yields a substantial crop of cricket balls.

A favourite story, told by Dr. Shaw, concerns an incident many years ago when, in a match, a ball was lofted over the wall and landed on the top deck of an open topped bus. The game was held up with the players hanging about waiting for the bus to come back from Ilkley with the ball! Incidentally, the late Milton Hudson, a former Vice President of the club, did not believe that story!

For some time, I recall, the practice included Dr. Doreen Tillotson and she lived in the house eventually occupied by Dr. Shaw.

The present Medical Centre, at Kirklands was opened in 1981 and recent retirements, after long and devoted service, were Dr. Colin Alexander and Dr. Graham Sherwood. Dr. John Thompson is now leader of an increasingly busy practice comprising Dr's Kenneth, Taylor, Young and Syed. They are well supported by receptionists.

Menston Hall or Low Hall

Miss Fletcher and Mr Laurence have both thoroughly explored the history of the Hall. Miss Fletcher takes us back a 1000 years in her book Menston Hall – the story of its Manor and site published in 1971. She describes the open field system – Rigg and Furrow – founded by the Anglo-Saxons. Each householder held from three to thirty strips of land on which to grow food for his needs, one strip remaining fallow each year.

In ploughing from end to end, the ground was thrown up in the middle and became raised as the plough came back on the other side, so a Rigg and Furrow layout was established which became more defined with the passing years.

Evidence of these strips can also be discerned on the Menston cricket field at the Fox. This can no doubt be verified by several cricketers who have misfielded a ball in the outfield!

In his splendid book A History of Menston and Hawksworth, Mr Laurence has established four generations of the Rhodes families to live at Low Hall, commencing with Richard who was born about 1625. He rebuilt the house in 1685 and died in 1703. The fourth and last Rhodes, John, did more rebuilding but had to mortgage the whole of his Menston estate to do so. He died a bachelor in 1751.

In 1753 the property was sold to Walter Hawksworth and remained part of the Hawksworth and Fawkes estate in Menston until 1876. During this period the Hall was a tenanted farm then it was sold by auction, by Dacre and Son to Mr James Padgett for £3050.

Mr Padgett was the owner of a flourishing woollen mill in Kirkstall and, at one time, is thought to have owned one of the mills in the Glen at Woodhead – possibly the Bleach Mill. The Padgetts were well respected in the village and the family drove to St. John's Church in their carriage and pair. In 1881 Mr Padgett, one of three patrons, had the Church decorated at his own expense.

The Hall was extended and parts were altered and rebuilt. It was surrounded by a high stone wall and a Lodge was built with fine gates and a driveway to the front door. The close proximity of the new Mental Hospital (Highroyds) no doubt prompted a decision to top the walls with cement and broken glass!

In 1914 we read in the *Wharfedale Observer*: 'The Menston Hall Estate, the property of the late Mr James Padgett was sold, by auction in the Hare and Hounds Hotel. The Hall itself, which had been unoccupied for several years, together with outbuildings, lodge, park and land covering 10¼ acres went for £1225 to Mr W P Butterfield'. A plot of 6½ acres adjoining the Hare and Hounds was also sold to Mr Butterfield for £505. This area is now Leathley Crescent and Avenue and is still often referred to as 'Butterfield's Estate'.

Included in the same sale were the Hare and Hounds, and Fox and Hounds Hotels and Menston Cornmill – part of the settled estate of the Fawkes family. The various pieces of land on offer were described as 'possessing extensive frontages to excellent and well frequented roads from which the Tolls have recently been removed'. The Hare and Hounds was bought by Mr Thomas Rushworth, a plumber of Shipley, for £2525. A note regarding the Fox and Hounds – sold to Mr John Carver of Bradford for £1360 – stated: 'From its proximity to the new station it presents a rare opportunity for the establishment of an hotel which cannot fail to be remunerative'.

Also in the sale were a number of Closes – Crooked Ing, Far Ing, Three Cornered Bit, Far Close, Carl Rain, High Ridding Close, Waitlands Close, Pease Croft, Great Rough Close, Hall Stead Close, Rainy Croft, Cross Butts Close, Greenlands Ing, Great Flat Close and Broadflat Close. Carl Rain, Hall Stead can be identified, Cross Butts Close is now the Cricket field and I believe Waitlands Close to be the area next to Carl Rain, going towards Burley.

Mr Butterfield was the owner of Butterfield Tank Works at Shipley and lived at Roseville at the top of Main Street (the junction of Moor

Lane and Bleach Mill Lane). It was said that, on the day of the sale the Hare and Hounds was filled with his employees – was this to minimise 'the opposition'? From humble beginnings, William P Butterfield built up the company which at one time employed 450 people manufacturing for a world-wide market, Road Tankers, Pressure Vessels, Storage Tanks and Galvanised Dustbins. The Hall was converted into two substantial residences; one half was occupied by Mr Robert D Cundall and the other half, the east end, by a Mrs Finnegan whom I remember as an elegantly dressed lady perambulating to St. John's Church on Sunday mornings.

Mr Cundall was also a successful business man. He was one of the first engineers to make and drive a car propelled by an internal combustion engine through the streets of Otley in 1896.

I recall Mr Butterfield as a dapper gentleman walking on Main Street with a stick and a flowered button hole to catch a bus at the Hare and Hounds to his Shipley Works. Sadly, in 1933, he was knocked down and killed crossing the road at the Hare and Hounds. Shortly after this, Mrs Finnegan having died, his son Clifford, his wife and family of four exchanged houses with the Cundalls. The next five years were spent refurbishing the house, outbuildings and garden. In 1936 there was a disastrous fire when a number of upper rooms were gutted and extensive damage done to decorations and furniture. The fire resulted in the Tower at the West end (built by Mr Padgett) being dismantled.

On the outset of the Second World War, the Hall was given over to the WVS for evacuees. The stables were equipped as an Ambulance Depot with an ambulance presented by Mr Butterfield. After the War, the Butterfields, retired to Beamsley and the Hall was converted into three luxury flats. In 1955 it was offered to, and accepted by, Ilkley Urban District Council for conversion into twelve less luxurious flats for old people. They were opened for residence in 1961.

Before the Council took over the Park as Menston's first Playing Field with two Tennis Courts, a Football Field and Children's Playing areas there had been a condition stipulated by Mr Butterfield that, if the club wished, it should be let at a nominal rent to Menston Cricket Club. With only an uneasy tenancy imposed by Whittakers at the Fox and Hounds, the Club's Committee gave Mr Butterfield's generous offer long and serious consideration. It was, however, eventually decided that the area was unsuitable for a cricket field.

The Garden of Remembrance was opened (for its short existence) in 1962. The surrounding wall was lowered to its present height and removed altogether on the Main Street side. In 1965 the Scout Hut and garages were constructed. During the late Sixties, the Lodge, stables and cottage in Farnley Road were demolished to make way for today's modern flats which were opened in 1969, and developed again in 2010.

A view of Menston Hall showing the tower built by James Padgett in 1876, and destroyed by fire in 1933.

Menston Hall today with additional buildings.

Menston Hall grounds – Miss Fletcher's evidence of the ancient 'Open field System' when each householder held from 3 to 30 strips of land sufficient to grow food for his needs. 1 of 3 strips to remain fallow each year.

Cottage in Low Hall Road demolished in 1961 to make way for the present Menston Hall flats.

The high wall which surrounded the Menston Hall Estate before being taken down in 1962.

The Lodge Menston Hall (junction of Farnley Road and Main Street) demolished 1969.

Kirklands

Kirklands, Main Street 1963 pre Community Centre showing the barn built at the time of an earlier house, possibly 300 years ago. This was originally Fourness house occupied by people of that name. Kirklands is a misnomer, having no connection with the Church. According to Miss E Lossel, an old Menstonian, the last private owners of the property were the Sowdens whose previous house in Halifax was called Kirklands and, regrettably I think, they preferred it to Fourness House.

For many years the house was owned by the Exleys, an old Menston family. Robert Exley was Menston's first JP, a prominent land owner and a founder of Menston's Methodist Society. The last Exleys to live there were two sisters (daughters of Robert) Ellen and Hannah who moved to Brookroyd opposite the Methodist Church in 1911.

Following the Exleys, Fourness House was the home of Ben Shaw a member of the Parish Council and father of Arthur a leading figure of Menston Cricket Club for the period between the wars. The Sowdens

The original Kirklands.

were the occupants during the thirties. During the Second World War, when the house was uninhabited, some of the rooms were used as a First Aid Centre. It was sold to Ilkley UDC in 1945. Kirklands became the 'Town Hall' and rooms were used as a Rate Office and a weekly Clinic for babies and toddlers. (Here, Mrs Elsie Walker gave loyal service weighing babies for two generations.) The Community Centre was added in 1973 thereby providing unrivalled facilities for sport and leisure activities.

Eric Caton, a former Chairman of the Retired Men's Forum, informs me there are some forty organisations in Menston and activities of twenty-seven of them take place in Kirklands.

The Library

Incorporated within the new Kirklands Community Centre was a new library – acknowledged to be one of the best in the district.

This replaced a string of earlier, makeshift, libraries going back to the early twenties when the first was combined with the Rate Office in what are now the newsagents at Lane Ends.

The Library, Community centre and Kirklands as it is today.

The Library Service – a County Service, was adopted by the Parish Council on the understanding that it would not increase the rates by more than a penny in the pound.

Harry Riding, the Menston Surveyor was the first librarian assisted by Maurice Baker. Next to accommodate the library was the tiny teacher's staff room in the Junior School and, after a short period, the books were moved to occupy one wall of a class room.

In 1936 Miss W E Voigt retired from the position of librarian after eleven years of service.

In 1937 we find the library moved yet again to Grove Road, with the Rate Office, in rooms attached to the Surveyor's House.

In 1947, ever growing in volume(s) as the village expanded, the library transferred to a ground floor room at Kirklands and thence to the new, purpose-built premises in the Community Centre in 1973.

Well established organisations making full use of Kirklands premises

The Community Association, which meets at Kirklands, was established in 1978. The inaugural meeting was chaired by Norman Hunt, a retired village policeman. A capacity audience of over 200 residents was addressed by Councillor Wyn Clavering and Dr. Eric Green, Chairman of the Burley Community Council formed some years previously.

One of the Council's earliest recommendations resulted in traffic lights being installed at the Hare and Hounds junction.

Over the years, blessed with dedicated chairman and committee members, though never fully appreciated or supported, the Council has been a vital element in the welfare of the village.

Outstanding contributions have been its watchful eye on the Green Belt, its concern with Leeds/Bradford Airport, its effect on Menston's environment and a continually updated Menston Guide.

Until recently, the Council was headed by Peter Ward and today, maintaining all its original aims, the Chairman is Alan Elsegood and the Secretary is the long serving Julia Bateson.

The Menston village design statement produced by the Community Association in 2000 is a splendid revue of Menston's evolution and it is hoped that it achieves all its objectives in caring for the future of our village. After 4 years Chairman Alan Elsegood was succeeded by Steve Ellams.

The Menston Annual Show

A Horticultural Society existed round about the 1920's and there was an annual show in the old Church Hall.

Its activities lapsed and it was not until 1975 that a group connected with St. John's Parish Church revived an interest in horticulture to establish today's popular Menston Show, held annually in Kirklands.

Four couples – the Hunts, the Fawcetts, the Husbands and the Pullans were mainly responsible.

Joan Pullan and Allan Husband were both active members until their untimely deaths – Joan in 1993 and Allan in 1994.

Since Joan's death, her husband John has successfully introduced a Gardener's Club which meets once a month at Kirklands.

The Evening Town's Women's Guild which has celebrated 30 years of activity.

The Bridge Club a well supported group which has met since 1975.

Monday Mixed Retirement Group has varied programmes including speaker illustrated lectures, a walking group and visits to places of interest. A similar group, established at the same time which met on Wednesday, sadly, was forced to disband due to a lack of organisers.

The Retired Men's Forum which meets fortnightly on Wednesday mornings. It was formed in 1974 by Frank Voight, a member of an old Menston family, and Vincent Hall. Past leading members have been Terry Roberts, Eric Caton and Ken Chadwick. Today's chairman is Steve Couling.

Widdon Burley Lane *(Photo Maurice Dakin).*

"Whiddon" Burley Lane Menston, built by Joshua Hart occupied for many years by the Pearson-Cravens and finally by the Sharpe family (W N Sharpe Printers – Classic Cards) demolished 1998 making way for 8, 5 bedroom houses, Whiddon Croft.

Willow Grove

Willow Grove – Park Road demolished 1982.

The last occupants of Willow Grove were Mr and Mrs Vernon Whitaker.

During the demolition in 1982, workmen came across what they thought to be a foundation or corner stone. The rock, being of Cornish granite, differed from the rest and a strange shape, such that it could have been locked in with stones on either side of it to form a secure course. The stone was chiseled with the words: – "Eddystone 1756".

The conclusion eventually reached as to why the stone is here, is that John Smeaton, the distinguished civil engineer who built Eddystone from 1756 to 1759, was a Yorkshire man. Storms in the winter months prevented landings on the rock and gave Smeaton opportunities for other undertakings one of which was making the river Calder navigable from Wakefield to Salter Hebble near Halifax.

For most of Smeaton's life, when not in London, he lived at Austhorpe Lodge, Whitkirk, four miles East of Leeds and it is quite conceivable that the stone is a memento of Smeaton's from Eddystone or the quarry near

Plymouth, and taken to Austhorpe Lodge although how it was moved the 20 miles from Leeds is unknown. 1333 AO cubic feet of masonry was used in the construction of Eddystone and the cost was £16,000.

The stone has been built into the wall forming the entrance to the present complex.

Willow Croft and Greystone Cottages in Park Road built on the site of Willow Grove.

Holly Bank

Holly Bank, Main Street for many years home of Dr. S. Edgerly former Medical Superintendent of High Royds hospital. The house was demolished in 1990 and the Ellicott Court complex was built on the site.

Holly Bank.

Ellicott Court.

Southbourne Cottage, Main Street

Deeds held by Mr. G. Galling, the present owner, are dated 8th June, 1773.

On 9th December, 1771 Walter Hawksworth, Lord of the Manor, and 6 others – Ann Hitch of York, Robert Harper of London, Mary Pulleyn of Burley, Joseph Heaton, Joseph Rhodes and John Pickard of Menston met for the purpose of dividing and enclosing a certain pasture or common called Menston Moor. The area was 320 acres, 2 roods.

At this time Joseph Heaton (carpenter) was living in Southbourne, possibly, the present Southbourne Cottage and the adjoining Ivy Cottage (Mrs. H. Hall) were one house.

Southbourne Cottage.

Menston's first Telephone Exchange was housed in Southbourne Cottage, Miss Mabel Woods was in charge. Later, round about 1930, the Exchange moved to Church View (opposite St. John's Church).

Following Miss Woods, Mrs. Kathleen Walker was telephonist/ caretaker until 1958. She was succeeded by Mrs. Peggy Burnett.

In 1960 the automatic telephone system was installed at White Cross, Guiseley.

Red House

Built in 1877 and in my memory occupied by Mr A. E. Hasse and Mr Andrew Young. It is now ground and first floor flats and, around, are attractive houses – Red House Gardens.

Red House, Cleasby Road.

Willow House Farm

Willow House Farm was owned at one time by Peates of Guiseley and, in my youth, rented by Harry Gill, a well known farmer and local sportsman.

Willow House Farm

In the outbuildings was the local slaughterhouse and, many years ago, in a wooden shop, by the roadside between Southbourne Cottage and the farm, was a butcher named Lee.

On this site was Menston's first school, provided by the will of Robert Moore, Rector of Guiseley in 1662.

From the History of the Ancient Parish of Guiseley by Philemon Slater – 1880:

'The School House referred to in the will and which is still used for the purpose of the school was built on part of the glebe land and kept in repair by the master. The land and the site of the buildings, devised for the school and master, form part of an estate at Menston which was sold by public auction in 1797 to the father of Robert Exley of Menston'.

Croft House, Main Street

Here lived Samuel Exley and in my memory, the Marjerisons (Harry Beaumont was their gardener living in the cottage opposite) and the Booth family.

For a few years the house was a residential hotel before being converted into flats in the fifties.

The house and stables (on the site of which now stand shops) were divided by a cobbled yard. The stables were used by John Turner's horses employed by the local Council.

There was a right of way through the cobbled yard which led down the field (now Croft Park) to a stile in the wall. Over the wall was a small wood, or coppice through which ran a stream and, a few yards beyond, was the path (now Fairfax Road) leading to the Railway Station. To reach this station footpath, one crossed the stream by a flat stone bridge. A continuation of this path from Croft House still exists and runs behind Fairfax Gardens into Westbourne Drive, over the railway bridge to Carlrayne.

Croft House.

Acacia House and a pre-fab cottage

Two more buildings of interest that disappeared are Acacia House by the "Fox" roundabout, replaced by a Morman Church and a pre-fab cottage in Main Street, owned by Ernest Firth and later, by Mr Clad. This was demolished in 1985 and on the site was built Moor View Croft.

Acacia House Menston was in its final years, a hotel.

Heather Court, St. Peter's Way

In March 2000, a public meeting, attended by Michael Portillo, Shadow Chancellor, revealed that Bradford Council proposed to close Heather Court – a wonderful community resource centre for the people of Menston and Burley for many years.

There was dismay, for both elderly residents and carers, when the Bradford Council Executive Committee confirmed their worst fears that the centre was to go on the property market. The land was estimated to be worth £700,000.

It was decided that users of the centre would be transferred to Menston Hall.

Numerous protesters inferred that the hall was in poor condition and totally unsuitable. Now, when the hall has been closed, it seems their fears were justified.

Heather Court is now a housing complex – Ling Court.

Pre-fab cottage in Main Street.

Kissing Gate

There were 2 of these gates on this path between the railway station and Lane Ends.

Fairfax Road (Station Fields)

These are two views of where what was known as Station Fields.

The top photo is now Fairfax Road, branching off Burley Lane, opposite St. John's church from Lane Ends, leading to the railway station – as the notice on the wall indicates.

The lower photo is the path in the opposite direction – the return route. St. John's Park houses can be seen in the distance. The path branching to the right, still existing, leads to Westbourne Drive and, over the bridge, to Carlrayne and Homestead.

Derry Hill

Mrs Baker's historical notes record that the row of cottages (left hand side going up) were known as Ashfield Place and owned by the Exleys. They were marked on the 1847 Survey as 'back to back'.

The front rooms were used for cottage weaving. Edward Lee, writing in 1924, (he came to Menston in 1862 as a boy of nine) 'I recall hand combing at the bottom of Derry Hill. Many evidences of this industry could be seen in the houses. Ceilings were black with smoke from the cinder fires in which the combs were treated.'

In 1871 the population of Menston decreased as machine looms in the mills superseded old cottage hand looms.

The two houses at the top of Ashfield Place were converted into shops – for Mrs Cowgill the village draper and, above, Joe Vickers the butcher.

Opposite, in a small wooden hut was Jack Walker the genial cobbler who took great pride in his shoe repairing. He succeeded Albert Bradley and the workshop was on the site of the original Working Men's Club built in 1921.

Further up the road (now number 23) was Fred Hopper's shop. He was a well loved greengrocer and, like Jack Reynolds, had a village 'round'.

Sam Barnard was another old Menston resident in Derry Hill. He was a builder and, at one time, employed by the Parish Council. He was regarded as an authority on the village drainage system.

On the opposite side (now number 22) lived the Clayton family. The house was an early village Post Office.

Beyond the junction with Walker Road was Thornby Place – three houses, and occupied in my youth, by the Shaw, Ayrton and Baker families (the row was extended to its present number of houses in two stages).

Bert Ayrton was the signalman at Menston Junction and, as boy's, he often welcomed us into his 'box' to watch him operate the signals.

Hillside

'Hillside' was a large Victorian house where now stands Hillside Court and was the home of Dr. J W Myers. In a remarkable career he trained as a textile designer then qualified as a barrister. Finally he became a medical practitioner and was hon. consultant at the Bradford Eye and Ear Hospital. Dr. Myers was a member of the Parish Council from 1919 to 1922.

The Quarry

The Quarry, now owned by Messrs. Clayax Yorkshire Stone Ltd., was an outcrop of sandstone and used in the building of many local cottages.

During the 1914-1918 War the quarry was used as a rifle range by the Menston Defence Volunteers 'to provide drill and instruction in the use of the rifle'. The initial membership of the club was over 200 and officers included Dr. Hyslop, C M Tankard, C W Bridgeland, C V Cawdry, W B Lee (the chemist) and H B Sutcliffe.

The Quarry eventually became the village rubbish tip and was declared 'almost filled' by Dr. Hyslop, the Chairman of the Sanitary Committee, in 1934.

Derry Hill Farm

Derry Hill Farm was called at one time Plane Tree Cottage. Fields grew barley and oats for making home brewed beer. In the field, above the quarry, was a malt kiln, used in the process.

The Pinfold and Old Blacksmith's Shop in Main Street

The Pinfold was an enclosure for stray cattle and sheep to be impounded. A well supplied water. At the time of its use, fines were imposed on owners of dogs which strayed at night time.

The Blacksmiths Shop, one of the oldest buildings in the village was in use as a Smithy 100 years until 1912 when the last blacksmith was Bill Hanson.

For a period the building was the village Fire Station and it fell into decay until 1937 when it was repaired by Ilkley UDC for use as a store.

In 1992, it was successfully converted into an attractive dwelling – Pinfold Cottage.

Dicks Garth Road

I do not know who 'Dick' was but this was the path that led to his garth or field.

In 1932, Councillor Henry Hargrave said that 'so many people had laughed at the name Dicks Garth Road' and suggested that it should be changed to Springfield Road. Thankfully, I think, the Council did not accede to his proposal – there must be a dozen Springfield Roads in Yorkshire but I'm sure, only one Dicks Garth.

Fairfax Hall

Fairfax Hall – originally Menston Old Hall – is, I think, Menston's major claim to historical fame.

Alastair Laurence and Elsie Fletcher have both dealt thoroughly with its fascinating story.

The Hall was the seat of Charles Fairfax from 1627 to 1672. It was here he and his wife Mary brought up their fourteen children and here, in the orchard, (contrary, I think, to Miss Fletcher's views) Oliver Cromwell planned the Battle of Marston Moor in 1644.

Amongst subsequent owners/tenants have been the Hawksworths, Joshua Hart (who changed the name to Fairfax Hall and who built Whiddon nearby), and the Jennings and Popplewell families.

In my youth the Hall was occupied by Major Maufe, later by Mr Robert Green, a timber merchant, and today's owners are Mr and Mrs Richard Wightman who are maintaining its proud tradition.

Menston Grange

Another fine example of Menston's architectural heritage is the Grange built in 1672. For many years it was two dwellings – the Grange on the left and Grange Farm on the right.

Fully researched by Alastair Laurence, he has established that the Grange was built for a high ranking church official, Robert Hitch of York.

The carved stone over the farmhouse door shows the date 1672 and the initials R.H.S. – those of Robert and Sarah Hitch.

The Farm was originally the village Court House and it has been suggested that the stones seen projecting from the right hand chimney were hanging stones from which summary justice was meted out!

Dominating tenancy and ownership down the years have been the Markham and Lupton families. The present owners of the Grange are Mr and Mrs Donald B Holdsworth. The farm was occupied by Mr and Mrs Ellison.

West end of Main Street. The immediate foreground is now occupied, on the left, by Grange Avenue and Moorview Croft. On the right is now Moorfield Avenue and recently built Rombalds Court (The courts of Menston Tennis Club were in this area).

The buildings shown are those of **Menston Laundry** with the manager's house adjoining. The Laundry was established from small beginnings by Mrs Eliza White, just after the First World War under the management of her son Richard (Dick), the firm expanded to employ over twenty people and serve a wide area outside the village.

In the next generation another Richard was the manager for many years before the business closed down in 1960.

Yorkshire Water eventually occupied the premises – until 1993, when the company moved to make way for Rombalds Court.

Menston Grange.

West end of Main Street c 1910.

Pinfold, Smithy/Firestation Main Street.

The pinfold was where, in the old days, stray cattle were impounded. At this time, fines were imposed if dogs were found straying at night.

Pinfold Cottage – conversion of the old smithy/firestation 1992.

Fairfax Hall.

October 1963 Main Street pre Heather Court and St. Peter's Way.

Three footpaths of a bygone era

October 1963 view from Main Street pre St. Peter's Way and Hawksworth Drive.

Footpath from the village to the station – now Fairfax Road.

Footpath – Station to the Fox & Hounds.

This is the footpath that led from the station to the Fox. The field on the left was, for many years the site for the annual Menston Feast. It is now Brooklands Estate.

The rear of Acacia House Hotel can be seen. It was demolished in 2003 to make way for the Mormon Church.

The cricket field, pavilion and the late Dr. Shaw's house are on the right with the Chevin in the background.

Well House and Eric Busby MBE

Menston oldest cottage, built about 1740 was bought, renovated and extended by Mr Eric Busby in 1963.

His description of the property and the adjoining Goosewell Fold is reproduced by permission of his daughter Mrs Pat Layfield.

Eric Busby was born in 1899 and was the last of the founder directors of the former Busby department store in Manningham Lane, Bradford. The store was taken over by Debenhams in 1958 and, at this time, employed some 1200 people.

Mr Busby left the family business at the age of sixty and founded the Lane Gallery in Bradford with the aim of providing opportunities to young professional artists (including David Hockney) to show their work.

He extended this work in 1967 at Goosewell Gallery which was underneath the house he built next to Well House (Goosewell Fold).

In the first four years nearly 2000 works by professional artists were shown here. He made no charge for the use of the premises, taking only commission on sales.

Later Mr Busby, at this own expense, restored the historic White Wells on Ilkley Moor, rescuing it from decay and vandalism.

In recognition of his public services he was made MBE in 1978.

He was a church warden for sixteen years at St. John's Parish Church and a founder of Menston Good Neighbour Service in 1970.

Well House

Until 1870 Menston Old Lane was a cart track called Goose Lane famous for primroses, wild strawberries and gooseberries. St. John's Park was a cornfield. Goose Lane led up to Derry Hill to the Gaping Goose Farm, the road from there to Hawksworth is still known as Goose Lane. The Parish Church was built in 1871, from then on, for fifty years Goose Lane, Menston, was known as Church Lane.

About 1890 the water rights from the spring on the East side of Well House were sold to the Otley Water Board, later the Ilkley UDC now the Bradford Metropolitan District Council, it is still named Gooseland Well on the charts of the water board – it is more correctly a basin catchment for three springs emerging from the high ground to the South, the supply is constant at 50,000 gallons per twenty-four hours, and is piped under the garden, through a tunnel under the railway to the covered reservoir.

Before 1890 a stream flowed through the garden of Goosewell Fold and served a pond of the reservoir – the original purpose of the tunnel will have been to provide a culvert under the railway line constructed in 1865.

Gooseland Well also supplied water for the bath in Well House, constructed about 1740, when it became fashionable to indulge in the hydropathical way of keeping fit. White Wells, Ilkley, was built during the same period.

Well House was first named 'Gooseland Well and Bath House' it was in use up to about 1865, the original building extended at a lower roof level to embrace the wall, the roof line can be traced on the East wall of the present building, there was a donkey stable on the West side, as also applied to the White Wells, Ilkley (An equivalent to the modern garage for a mini).

Well House is almost certainly on the line of a Roman road that communicated with the fort of Olicana, whilst it is incorrect to designate the baths at Well House or White Wells as Roman, it is probable that both sites were used by the Romans who valued spring water for bathing and drinking.

Well House is believed to be the oldest cottage property in Menston, it remained in a primitive state until 1963 when the bathroom and kitchen wing were added. It was during the 1963 alterations that the old bath was discovered this had been filled in and flagged over about 100 years ago, and forgotten.

Some relics of under floor hot air heating were traced to the remains of a brick furnace outside the building. The present dining area was the changing room in bath house days. There is evidence of the cottage having been used for weaving in the stone door frame built into the wall on the South side.

Goose Lane is known to have been a pack horse route linking with Goose Eye, Keighley, and onwards to Halifax, which was the most important Northern centre for delivery of cottage woven cloth, sold at the famous Piece Hall (now renovated) in Halifax. About the middle of the last century Well House became a farmstead, and was successfully worked by the Turner family, until, year by year more and more agricultural land was swallowed up for building.

Goosewell Fold and Art Gallery

Built in 1967. Occupying the land previously used for wooden farm buildings. The new property is constructed in Gloucestershire hand thrown brick, with old stone roof to a rake which agrees with Well House, the object being to convey an appearance of oldness and belonging which will be more apparent in twenty years. It is hoped that Goosewell will continue to give pleasure as a private dwelling, and a centre for visual art and music, and be saved from any development which might spoil the atmosphere of this corner of old Menston.

Well House Menston *(Photo Alastair Lane).*

Goosewell Gallery.

PARISH COUNCILS, SCHOOLS AND CHURCHES

Councils and Councillors

1894 was an important year for Menston – Parish Councils came into being and the new Board School (the present Junior School) was opened. Miss Fletcher has described how the village was governed from medieval times by the Lord of the Manor, Courts Leet and Baron, overseers and a Justice of the Peace.

These regimes ceased with the Local Government Act of 1894 when both Urban and Rural District Councils were formed. Small parishes were grouped together under RD Councils. Where a parish had over 300 inhabitants, there was a Parish Council, and a Parish Meeting for less than 300.

The Wharfedale RDC consisted of twenty parishes and Menston was the only one with two representatives.

The first Parish Council elections were held on 15th December 1894 and, in Menston where the population was 1742 (including inmates and staff of the Asylum), there were no fewer than twenty-one candidates willing to serve.

Jabez Cole was one of Menston's leading lights at this time, a Methodist, a prominent land owner and the Cole in the eventual partnership of coal merchants, Smith, Parkinson and Cole. He had built for himself and members of his family several large, imposing houses in Cleasby Road and Main Street. Jabez gave the land to Messrs Joseph Gill on which to construct Bleach Mill Lane – the road leading to the Rombalds Moor Bleach Works at Woodhead, on the understanding that he should supply coal to the mill. The Parish Council existed for forty-two years (1895-1937) during which time Dr. J W Hyslop served for thirty-three years, Mr Charles M Tankard served a total of twenty-five years and Mr H B Sutcliffe for twenty-five years. Dr. Hyslop, the founder of today's medical practice, commenced his long connection with Menston at Newfield Lodge at the foot of Cleasby

Road. He later married the daughter of Jerimiah Whittaker, the brewer, who had 'Aintrees' built (in Cleasby Road) incorporating a surgery, as a wedding present.

MENSTON
PARISH COUNCIL
ELECTION.
Form of Ballot Paper.

Find the name of COLE on the Voting Paper and mark a X opposite the name, as below.

1	Brookes, James Edwin	
2	Brotherton, Charles	
3	Clapham, John	
4	Clayton, John	
5	COLE, JABEZ	X
6	Cowling, Mark	
7	Crowther, Joseph	
8	Dolby, James	
9	Hardaker, Joshua	
10	Hartley, Charles James ..	
11	Hart, Joshua	
12	Hunt, Herbert	
13	Jobling, Theophilus	
14	McDowall, John Greig ..	
15	Mackereth, William	
16	Oddy, Benjamin	
17	Padgett, Philip	
18	Popplewell, Christopher Jennings ..	
19	Rayder, John	
20	Tankard, Charles Matthew	
21	Watkinson, William	

In soliciting your Vote for the Parish Council, I assure you that if I am returned as a Councillor, I shall faithfully watch over the real interests of the inhabitants, and secure any needful improvement, but shall strongly oppose any useless and extravagant outlays of the public money.

COLE.

MENSTON
PARISH COUNCIL
ELECTION.

Burgess No. ....

Name ....

Address ....

You Vote at the
OLD BOARD SCHOOL.

Please make a mark thus X opposite the name of
JABEZ COLE
As below:

COLE, JABEZ.	X

VOTE EARLY
Poll Opens at 8-o a.m. and Closes at 8-o p.m.

VOTE EARLY
AT THE
OLD BOARD SCHOOL.

Poll Opens at 8-0 a.m. and Closes at 8-0 p.m.

The Doctor was elected to the Parish Council in 1904.

Yours faithfully,
Jabez Cole.

MENSTON PARISH COUNCIL.

To the ELECTORS OF MENSTON.

Ladies and Gentlemen,

Having been asked by a large and most influential number of Ratepayers to become a Candidate for the above, and also nominated at the Ratepayers' Meeting, I have real pleasure in complying with their wishes.

I am, and have been a resident in the Parish for many years, am a large ratepayer, and well known. I feel deeply interested in the welfare of the Parish, and, having plenty of leisure time I shall, to the utmost of my ability, keep down the rates as low as possible, convenient with efficiency, and shall watch the interests of the Parish as a whole.

I trust you will honour me with your votes on **Saturday next, December 15th, 1894,** and, if elected, I trust that the confidence you bestow on me will not be misplaced.

I am, Ladies and Gentlemen,

Yours obediently,

JABEZ COLE.

Rose Mount,
Menston, Dec. 8th, 1894.

Printed and Published by John Dale & Co., Bridge Street, Bradford.

Jabez Cole Parish Council Election.

He reported that in 1912, there were no cases of infectious diseases and Menston had pure, bracing air and a good sanitary system. 'I do not think any township in the whole valley can beat Menston as a health resort or for residential purposes for the good of one's health', he said. At the final meeting of the Parish Council in 1937 he regarded the amalgamation with Ilkley as 'an act of tyranny'.

Charles M Tankard, first elected in 1896, I remember as a tall upright gentleman who lived at 'Ingle Nook' in Cleasby Road. He took an active interest in numerous Menston Societies including the Cricket Club to which he was elected a life member in 1943.

Herbert B Sutcliffe lived at Fieldhead in St. John's Park. He was manager of Bradford Telephone Exchange and his telephone number was MENSTON 1.

The members of the last Parish Council were: A C Voigt, Dr. J W Hyslop, H B Sutcliffe, A Weightman, H Brown, H Hargrave, A Outtersides, A S Maston and J E Roberts. The final meeting of the Wharfedale RDC was held in Otley in March 1937. At this time, Henry Longden (Chairman), Henry Hargrave, and H B Sutcliffe were Menston's representatives. From 1937 to 1974 Menston and Burley were absorbed into Ilkley Urban District Council. Incidentally, transference to a new authority meant a rate increase from 2 to 11 old pence in the pound.

Henry Hargrave, Colin Outtersides and Janet Ellicott all served as Chairman of the Council. Fred Atkinson and Harry Bell represented the village for many years. In 1974, with the reorganisation of local government, Menston, Burley and Ilkley came under the authority of Bradford Metropolitan Council.

In 1981-82 Joan Beevers had an outstanding year of office as Lady Mayoress of Bradford. Wyn Clavering gave her time and energy to Council and Community affairs for several years before she and husband Colin left the district.

The village has been well served, irrespective of party politics, by representatives like Peter Williams, Joyce Galling, Iris Carney, former chairman Audrey Brand and recent Bradford Lord Mayor, Richard Wightman. Dale Smith represents Rombalds Ward on the Bradford

Metropolitan Council and takes an active interest in several village organisations – including scouts and guides. Community Association, singing groups and cricket club.

Dale is also chairman of the primary school governors and the executive committee responsible for the running of Abbeyfield – the elderly peoples home in Cleasby Road which he helped to establish with Mr H K Thompson in 1977.

In December 2010 residents were transferred to a magnificent new development – The Beeches. Farewells were expressed to the retiring staff – Margaret and Irvin Grice, Sandra Johnson, Judith Hennessay, Dreda Lacey and Barbara Svensgaard.

Beginning in 2002 there were meetings of various authorities as to whether Menston and Burley should break away from Ilkley UDC and form their own parish councils.

Menston community council became involved and numerous expressions by the public – for and against.

Finally, in 2006, having permission from the Secretary of State a new Menston Parish Council was formed. The chairman elected was Peter Finaly MBE and the chairman of the new planning committee was Gordon Metcalf. The first meeting was held in the scout hut in Low Hall Road in May 2006.

Some notes regarding Menston's early activities in politics

The Unionists were in existence in 1909 when a party travelled to Bolton Abbey by waggonette.

Amongst the members were Mr and Mrs Daniel, Mr A. Daniel, Mr C. W. Bridgeland, Mr George Rimmington, Mr and Mrs W. Harland and Mr and Mrs J. E. Bowden.

They met in 1922 with an object to maintain the British Constitution of the King and Parliament to uphold the bond of Empire and Imperial Unity. Member's subscription was 1/- (5d). J. E. Boden was Chairman and the Committee included H. Longden, R. D. Cundall and J. Shields.

Familiar names on the Committee in 1922 were Arthur Voigt, Walter Fletcher, Mark Bateson, Dr. Myers and Charles M. Tankard.

In 1924 J. E. Roberts, C. Broadwith, Bert Oliver, G. Terry, Sam Barnard and Sam Oddy were committee members. Sixty members attended a Pie Supper at the Malt Shovel Hotel in October 1933 (Entrance 1s/-, Supper 1s/-).

Entertainment was provided by Alfred Biss, Baritone and Tom Gill pianist. The event was attended by the local M.P. J. Horace Lockwood.

There were no meetings between 1939 and 1943 but the Association was revived at the end of 1944 when the President was R. D. Cundall, Chairman W. F. Shepherd, Secretary Stanley Wright, Treasurer Stanley Ryley. Committee included J. H. Ellicott, J. Hoffman, G. Mackrell, G. W. Briggs, and Dr. R. J. Gourlay.

The annual subscription was revised to 2s/6d (12 ½ p). The Liberals formed an Association in the village in 1910.

The first annual report stated that 'interest had been considerably revived' with a membership of sixty-one.

Amongst the officers were T. G. Greig, Ben Shaw, J. Robinson, C. J. Hartley, Professor A. W. Gineve, F. W. Goodall and James Maston.

SCHOOLS IN MENSTON

TIMEPLAN

1622	At Willow House Farm, Main Street in an out building Founded by Rev. Robert Moore Rector of Guiseley.
1797	This school continued to educate the children of Menston.
1826	This school was now called The Academy.
1831	The Wesleyan Methodists opened a new building (Now Mr Waite's building) as a Sunday School and Day School.
1860's	The Anglicans started a Sunday and Day School for Anglican children in a cottage in Derry Hill, number 37. This cottage was also a church until St. John's was opened in 1871.
1873	A National Church of England School was opened at Lane Ends.
1887	The Wesleyan Day School was closed and the children joined the New Board School.
1887	The new Board School opened in Lane Ends (Now Parmley Graham) this was managed by a Board made up of Anglican and Wesleyan Church members.
1889	The Wesleyan Day School was used by the Infant Board School.
1894	The Board School at Lane Ends closed.
1894	The New Board School opened in Main Street on the present site to take both infant and junior pupils. It cost £4, 910 to build.
1967	The New Infant School was opened and infants went to the St. Peter's Way site leaving the juniors in the Junior School.
1981	Junior School threatened with closure – Parents Action Group formed to fight closure – they win.
1986	Junior School threatened with closure – Parents Action Group formed to fight closure – they win a reprieve on closure of the

Junior School and the Infant school becoming a first school. On 5th December, Councillors in Bradford settled on combining the Junior and Infant Schools to form one school, Menston Primary.

1992 The Junior and Infant Schools join to form Menston Primary School.

1994 Menston Primary School celebrates its Centenary in the Junior building.

2000 Menston Primary School leads the celebration in the school grounds of the New Millennium, the Main Road being closed to traffic for a Street Party.

Pat Reid

The Council or Junior School

The present Junior School was opened in 1894. It was built on former common land used for waste and livestock before the Enclosure Acts of 1770. This area separated the two ends of the village and it is interesting to note that in my young days we often had football and cricket matches – 'Villagers V T' other Enders' and the dividing line was the school.

Before the new school there were Church Schools: Wesleyan and Church of England operating on both weekdays and Sundays.

The Wesleyans had a school as early as 1832; the building is now occupied by Messrs Waites Joiners and Undertakers. Joseph Clough was the master and lived in the house adjoining. He paid £3 a year rent to the chapel trustees but kept the proceeds from the pupils who paid either 2d or 4d per week.

Some thirty years later, according to Miss Fletcher, a 'zealous curate' Mr Collins from Burley commenced day classes for C of E children in a house in Derry Hill.

Edward Lee who came to Menston in 1862 as a boy of 9 wrote: 'A Mr Jackson was the Schoolmaster; one corner of the room was curtained off for sleeping quarters for himself. My teacher was Exley Peate son of the late Tom, brother of Jonathan, Caleb and William Peate' (Guiseley mill owners).

This house – third from the top, left hand side going up, also served the Anglicans for Sunday worship until St. John's was opened in 1871. The school eventually moved to purpose built premises on the site of the former Church Hall at Lane Ends now used for industrial purposes. In 1886 the Ministry of Education ordered an election of a School Board and to close the Church Schools. There was some opposition to a Board School by rate-payers who pointed out that the cost to upkeep the Church School was an 8d rate whereas the 'imposition' of a Board School would involve a rate of 2/- in the pound. By thirty-one votes to one a meeting rejected the proposal of a compulsory rate for a Board School.

However, the Ministry had its way and a non sectarian school the National School – was formed. The older children attended the old Church School at Lane Ends and the Wesleyan School was used for infants until the building of the new Board School in 1894.

The 'Board' consisted of five local worthies: Adolphus Calvert, Samuel Hall (Vicar), Ernest Otto Voigt, Joseph Exley and Edward Willis.

The newly elected Board appointed a Mr and Mrs Bryning of Ashby-de-la-Zouch as headmaster and headmistress with salaries of £100 and £40 per annum respectively and according to the *Wharfedale and Airedale Observer*, there were 280 applicants for the positions.

By the time of the new school being occupied, Mr Frederick Perry and his wife were head teachers. Mr Perry was a popular master and, according to an old scholar Vic Bilton, was a 'strict disciplinarian but a fair chap'.

Following Mr Perry in 1920 as headmaster was Alfred S Maston who came from Otley. He was another strict but fair disciplinarian and widely respected in and out of school. Mr Maston served for many years as a Parish Councillor and a member of several village societies including the Methodist Church (as a local preacher) the Cricket Club and British Legion. As a teacher he gave a first class grounding in the three Rs. Many former pupils will recall the English lessons and the fascinating introductions he gave to the works of Conan Doyle, Charles Kingsley, Robert Louis Stevenson and other literary giants.

I think of Mr Maston when I hear 'Jerusalem' which we sang in assembly before departing school on Friday evenings.

Coupled with Mr Maston, generations of Menston school children will remember another loveable personality – Miss Alice Jennings or 'Peggy' as she was affectionately known. Travelling each day from Guiseley by train; Miss Jennings was one of my teachers in the late twenties. When she retired in 1962, after forty years in the same school, she was teaching my daughter Moira with the same care and dedication.

A history of the Village School was compiled by a former teacher, David Preston to commemorate the Centenary of the present school.

Menston Junior School.

Church House No. 37 Derry Hill.

This house was used by Menston Anglicans both as a Day School and for Sunday worship before the school at Lane Ends and St. John's Church were built.

The Old Church Hall, Lane Ends.

The old Church Hall, built in 1906, as well as being a Sunday school and an early day school, served as the village hall for many years before the Kirklands Community Centre was built in 1973.

Under the wall, facing Derry Hill, there used to be a long seat made from railway sleepers. During long summer evenings the seat accommodated several old village worthies, amongst whom were Joe Emmott, Billy Diskin, a former employee of the Bleach Mill, Tommy Bolton who kept bantam hens and supported Bradford City and Billy Leyburn who, for perhaps 30 years, was responsible for the delivery of Sunday newspapers in the village. (He was eventually succeeded in this capacity by Colin Newstead and later Leslie Wood).

Menston School c. 1921 or 1922. **Left to Right – *Back row:*** Jack Butler, Mark Richmond, Billy Simpson, Jack Thornton, Horace Wood, Billy Shaw, Jake Smith, Hubert Reynolds. ***2nd row:*** Mr Perry, Winnie Smith, George Jefferson, David Rawnsley, Harry Hollings, Herbert Rhodes, Francis Chipman, Charlie Roberts, Edith Weir. ***3rd row***: Edith Kempton, Kathleen Greenwood, Lily Reynolds, Nellie Lancaster, Mary Davey, Emily Dyson, Evelyn Broadhead, Iris Hawkes, Vera Spivey. ***4th row***: Phylis Hannam, Gwen Morse, Gladys Atkinson, Violet Fitzpatrick, Mary Weightman, Nellie Garforth, Marie Jeffray, Winnie Fillingham.

... Jack Hill, John Allewell, Stanley Ayrton.

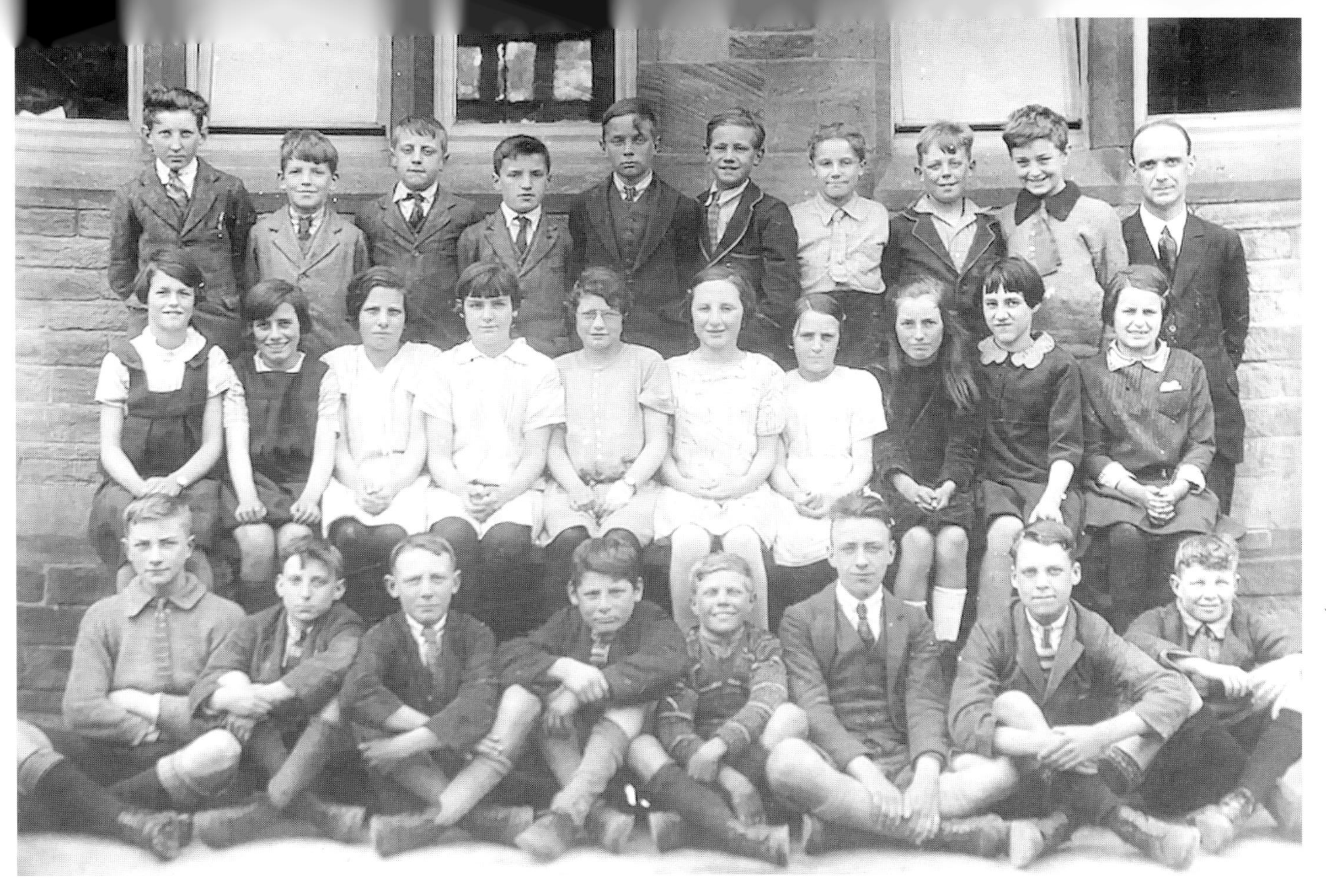

Menston School c. 1927 *(Photo: Mrs P Hammond)*. **Left to Right** – ***Back row***: Ernest Pullan, Billy Murray, Herbert Turner, Herbert Walker, Claude Wilkinson, Jim Brooking, Jack Morse, Roland Threapleton, Amos Edmondson, Mr Maston. ***2nd row***: Irene Bennett, Phyllis Hill, Grace Jackson, Olive Moxon, Dolly Dennison, Mary Hargreave, Doris Mudd, Audrey Walker, Mary Allewell, Millie Christian. ***Front row***: Eric Gibson, Dick Weatherhead, Richard White, Mark Appleby, George Windle, Jack Armitage, George Spivey, David Atkinson.

Menston School 1930. **Left to Right** – ***Back row***: Miss Downey, Dick Hargrave, Fred Walker, Leslie Wood, Jeffray Weightman, Alan Jennings, Billy Youill, Dennis Cowgill, Billy Dibb, Tom Wild. ***2nd row:*** Irene Walker, Elsie Holdsworth, Mary McKinley, Alice Glaister, Doreen Glover, Marjorie Windle, Eileen Turner, Molly Parker, Olive Armitage, Joan Wright. ***3rd row:*** Stella Claughton, Kathleen Geary, Mary Atkinson, Gwyneth Branch, Elsie Spivey, Jessie Barnard, Muriel Dawson. ***Front row***: Kenneth Beaumont, George Reynolds, Stanley Atkinson, Jack Walker, George Tennant.

Menston School 1932. **Left to Right** – ***Back row***: Billy Normandale, Edwin Foulger, Jack Kell, Fred Walker, Harry Jennings, Charlie Dolby, Edmund Weightman, Donald Hancock, Jack McKinlay, Desmond Dale, Dennis Gledhill. ***2nd row:*** Peter Robinson, Donald Reynolds, Alfred Hudson, Elsie Holdsworth, Marjorie Brown, Marjorie Settle, Mary Blackburn, Joan White, Kenneth Beaumont, Kenneth Gibson, Mr. Maston. ***3rd row***: Kenneth Maston, Sylwin Staziker, Irene Sykes, Violet Pilkington, Mary Barnard, Olwyn Davies, Joan Heaton, Annie Hancock, Olive Fitzpatrick, Fred Brooking. ***Front row:*** Wilson Wright, Dennis Windle, Leslie Pilkington, Herbert Braithwaite, John Heaton, Ernest Holdsworth, Bobby Wigglesworth, Joe Emmott, Jack Biss.

Menston School 1932. **Left to Right** – ***Back row:*** Leonard Kell, Kenneth Settle, Donald Woodhead, Herbert Hudson, Ronald Walker, Dennis Turner, Edgar Turner, Phillip Armitage, Norman Turner, Colin Newstead, Colin Outtersides, Cyril Blackburn. ***2nd row:*** Kathleen Braithwaite, Jean Mansfield, Joyce Windle, Iris Rawnsley, Gladys Mudd, Audrey Mallinson, Marjorie Tennant, Peggy White, Nerys Claughton, Phyllis Smith, Lucy Reynolds, Sylvia Biss, Joan Dale, Betty Wright. ***3rd row***: Marie Hancock, Vera Pickard, Florence Wigglesworth, Betty Watson, Ethel Taylor, Dorothy Land, Vera Windle, Glover, Mary Haliday, Alice Staziker. ***Front row:*** Teddy Christian, Geoffrey Bolton, Maurice Carlton, Gordon Biss, Jack Land, Peter Frizell, [illegible] Robert Normandale, Douglas Biss, Gordon Newton.

21st July 1953 the occasion was the retirement of Mr A S Maston Headmaster of the junior school for 30 years. The presentation of a writing bureau to Mr Maston was made by Miss Alice (Peggy) Jennings herself a teacher at the school for 40 years..

Crowning of the May Queen Ceremony. The queen was Moira Kell (the author's daughter) Menston school 1964.

St Mary's Catholic School

St Mary's opened its doors for the first time as a comprehensive school in 1964, when pupils from the surrounded areas first attended. It was officially opened in 1965 by the Rt. Rev. Mgr. George Patrick Dwyer, Bishop of Leeds. In 2000 it became a specialist sports college and in 2013 became an Academy. In its 50 years history, under various head teachers it has gained a high reputation in both academic studies and various sports. The school also boast the fact of having quite a number of pupils that have gone on to become celebrities in the world of entertainment, most notably, Matthew Lewis who played Neville Longbottam in the Harry Potter films and Simon Rix, Nick Baines and Nick Hodgson of Kaiser Chiefs fame.

Village Churches

In my youth, it seemed to me that apart from the God they worshipped, members of Menston's Churches had little in common.
T'Churchers and t'Chapelers geographically close enough, hardly ever met except at Remembrance services and perhaps at concerts produced by each church.

The Catholic Church, built in 1933, seemed so remote from the village and nearer Burley than Menston.

The Congregational Church – opposite Kirklands in Main Street had only a short existence – 1907 to the mid-thirties.

Changes came in 1963 when, at a national level, discussions took place between Anglicans and Methodists with a view to creating greater unity between their churches. Rev. Michael Heckingbottom and Rev. Stanley Rose were instrumental in the formation of the local Council of Churches which comprises the three Menston churches and those in Burley.

The joint Christmas card first appeared in 1963 and there was a history making service at St. John's on 30th November, 1972, when Anglicans and Methodists took communion together for the first time. Furthering the cause of unity, the Scouts and Guides became jointly sponsored at this time.

Ecumenically, great strides were made during the incumbencies of Rev Peter Gray and Rev John Ward with joint services and social get-togethers.

The early years of both the Anglican and Methodist Churches have been documented. In 1986, I produced a brief history of Methodism in Menston (coinciding with the centenary of the present church) and in 1971, Mrs Jean Heckingbottom compiled a remarkable account of the first hundred years of St. John's. Copies of both books exist in Menston's and other local public libraries.

Marking the centenary of the Parish Church, the Lady Chapel and Choir and Vestry extensions were opened in 1971. Part of the cost of £13,000 emanated from a fund created by Stanley Ryley in memory of his wife, Marjorie, who died in 1947. Appropriately, the Ryley's eldest son, Michael, was the architect of the building.

In 1972 it was decided that the old Church Hall, though serving the community in a variety of ways, including a Sunday School, a Youth Club and main Village Hall, was too lofty, too old and too expensive to maintain.

Ideally situated at Lane Ends for easy access (a fact no doubt realised later by the Church Authorities) it was thought that the building would become under used with the opening of the Community Centre at Kirklands.

The old Hall was sold to Parmley Graham, a light engineering firm who retained the outward appearance of the building.

Mr Norman Sharpe* who lived at 'Whiddon' a large house close to the old Vicarage, gave a plot of land adjoining the Church and the new Parish Room was built, at a cost of £21,850. It was dedicated by the Bishop of Bradford the Rt. Rev. Ross Hook in January, 1978.

---

*Footnote: Mr Sharpe died in 1987 leaving a total of over £2m in his will. Amongst local beneficiaries were Menston Darby and Joan Club and the Scouts and Guides who each received £500.

St. John's Parish Church.

Menston's two Methodist churches built in 1826 and 1886.

Tying the Parish Church gates at Wedding Ceremonies

An old village custom perhaps dating back to the consecration of the church in 1871.

The gates are tied during a wedding ceremony and the bride and groom are not allowed to leave until coins are thrown to local children gathered outside.

Traditionally, the gates are tied with string and it needs only a pair of scissors, usually carried by the best man, to effect an opening when coins have been thrown.

From time to time, there has been the possibility that the custom would be stopped by the church council. Older, less well behaved children have used wire instead of string to tie the gates.

Mrs Jean Heckingbottom, wife of a former vicar, reported in 1980, that 'children have become bored with waiting for the bridal party to appear, fighting has broken out, cars are damaged and the more boisterous children climb a street lamp post and trample over the graveyard'.

Tying the church gates at the wedding of Jean and Keith Terry.

St. John's Girls Friendly Society

This group of girls prospered in the thirties under the enthusiastic and motherly Mrs Hodd, wife of Vicar F A Hodd (1922-1937).

They were trained in ballet, dramatic art and verse speaking. Winning diocesan competitions in Bradford, they reached the All England Finals and competed in London.

Methodism had is beginnings in Menston as early as 1744 and the first chapel built in 1826 still exists now as an artists studio at Lane Ends.

Marking the Centenary of the present church in 1986, during the Ministry of Rev. J Douglas Wood, the entrance vestibule was successfully enlarged within the existing structure at a cost of £18,000.

Menston's St. John's G.F.S. c1930.

Back row: June Oldman, Miss Axom, Dorothy Turner.
Middle row: Gwneth Branch, Betty Barnard, Alice Turner, Mary Weightman.
Front row: Elsie Spivey, Sylvia White, Kathy White.

The Old Sunday School

Some of my first recollections are associated with the Old Sunday School in Main Street.

Leading Morning School was local headmaster Mr A S Maston. The Primary Department, in the afternoon, was conducted by Rene Myers and Alice Bell. Class teachers were Margaret Baker, Winnie Fillingham and Belle Moon. Advancing to Junior status, Sunday afternoon classes were held in the corners of the Church. Superintendents were Laurie Mellor, Gordon Holmes and Maurice Baker. Bobby Knox and Fred Bateson were class teachers.

As primitive as the building was, it provided all that was necessary for Sunday worship and social events – concerts, teas and Sunday School parties. These were splendid occasions with games arranged by Mr Fred Holland who had a natural gift for entertaining children.

During the week, there were evenings with a magic lantern and Band of Hope meetings which gave ample scope to local talent in the entertainment world.

The Band of Hope, led by Mr Harry Brown and Mr and Mrs Harry Beaumont, was eventually succeeded by the Rechabites – a sort of junior Masonic Lodge. The numerous officials were addressed as 'Brothers' and 'Sisters' and wore sashes. The movement was inaugurated by a Mr Kane who came from the Bradford 'Tent'. The meetings were generally of a social nature but a more serious aspect, like the Band of Hope, was the condemnation of strong drink.

Whitsuntide was always an important weekend in a young Methodist's calendar. Sunday was the day for 'showing off' new clothes and the culmination of many weeks of rehearsal under Mr Bell for a Service of Song and Recitation. The Rev. T O C East came to conduct the service and present the prizes for good attendance. My own particular literary 'gem' was 'The Celandine', which was gabbled off with eyes fixed rigidly on the gallery clock.

Whitmonday was another exciting day. The morning was devoted to watching the Annual Bradford *Telegraph and Argus* Walk, when, it seemed, the whole village assembled on the main road between the 'Hare' and the 'Fox'.

The afternoon was the Sunday School 'Treat' or Sports Day in Mr Harry Gills's field (behind Willow House farm). For the girls, ropes were suspended from tall trees to make swings. Thistles would be scythed and cow claps avoided for the boys to play a makeshift cricket match, 'Villagers v T'other enders'. There were races for all ages and parents also had the opportunity to display their Olympic talents.

At tea time there were sandwiches and buns from bottomless paper bags and thick, brown tea dispensed from a bright copper urn into solid china mugs clearly marked 'Menston Wesleyan Chapel'.

The Methodist church. A Sunday school group in 1942.

Left to right – *Standing:* ---, Maurice Baker, Cyril Jordan, Jack Kell, Robert Normandale, Leslie Pitts, Alan Coupland, Richard Atkinson, Harry Pitts. ***Seated:*** Gladys Baker, Nancy Benson, Gloria Powell, Connie Benson, Dorothy Jordan, Diane Grimshaw, Mary Halliday, Kathleen Webb, Betty Marshal, Barbara Kell.

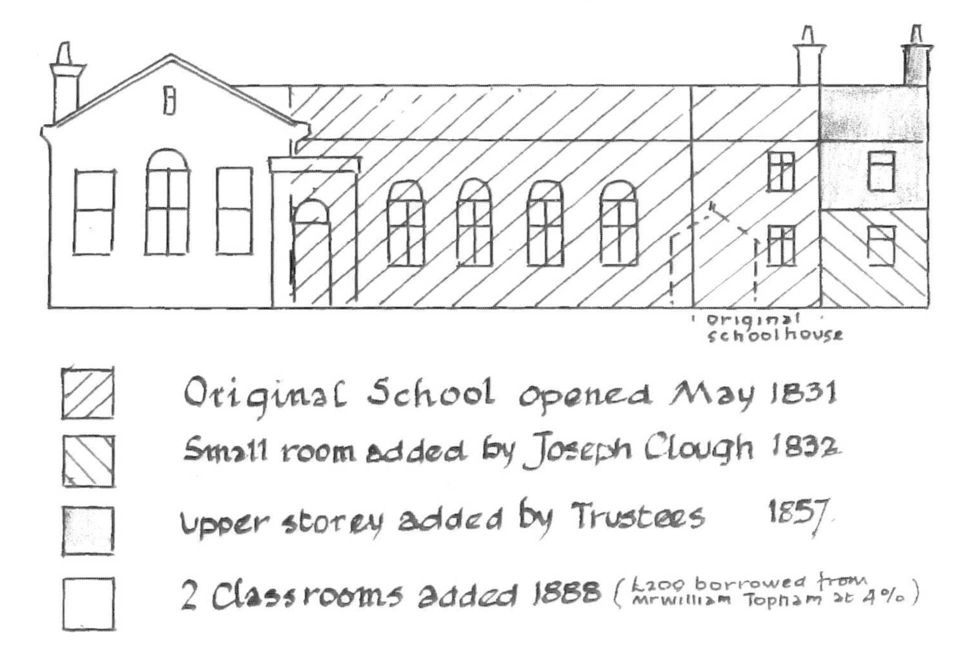

Diagram showing the development of the Wesleyan Sunday / Day School.

Then, as the shadows lengthened and evening came, the cricket match was won and lost and the last race run, we gathered at the farmhouse door to express our thanks to Mr and Mrs Gill. We sang their favourite hymns – Now the Day is Over and The Day Thou Gavest, Lord, is Ended.

In 2003 our village churches were blessed with their first female ministers. Rev. Ruth Yeoman joined St. John's Parish Church and Rev. Fiona Spandler was appointed to the Methodists.

They both involve themselves with local organisations, they are known by their Christian names and, I feel, an asset to the village.

The first school master was Joseph Clough – he paid the church trustees £3 a year rent and charged his pupils 4p a week.

In 1846 he was replaced by Edward Hinchcliffe who was master for 8 years.

A Mr Peacock was master until 1857 when Mr Clough returned. He lent the trustees £30 to add the upper storey to the school house. The building ceased to be a day school in 1894 when the new Elementary school was

Former Wesleyan Sunday/Day school, Main Street.

The Congregational Church, Main Street, (opposite Kirklands) built in 1907.

built but continued as a Sunday school until 1933 when the Methodists opened their new school premises behind the church.

The old school served as a village hall for many years (until St. John's church hall built in 1907) it was sold in 1935 to Mr Arthur Biss (for £450) for industrial purposes (Burling & Mending). Before being acquired by the present owners Messrs Waite (1958) the property was used by Mr Harry Corbett as the famous Sooty's workshop.

The Congregational Church

Rev. G H Brown was its popular minister and local families attending were: – Richmonds (Lucy was the last organist), Cowlings, Joblings, Stradlings, Cowgills, Waites, Richardson (Clarence Drive), Little (Elmete Grange), Patterson.

One of my earliest memories of the church is a series of lively meetings in the thirties, conducted by an American Evangelist, Mrs McKenzie Mentiply.

Before the building was closed in the sixties, it was used as a private school – Norway Lodge.

Norway Lodge was the name of the house – one of four – opposite the Fox and Hounds where the school originated. It was run by two very dignified ladies, the Misses Maunder.

A Mormon church appeared, next to the Fox and Hounds, replacing the Acacia House Hotel, demolished in 2003.

The Catholic Church, opened in 1932, in Bradford Road to serve Menston and Burley.

It was dedicated to S S John Fisher and Thomas More.

TRANSPORT AND EARLY INDUSTRY

Transport

THE LATE Mrs Lucy Storr a Menstonian, recalled, in her younger days, before the age of motor transport, the Horse Bus owned by Jeffray Jennings, which travelled to Otley market from Lane Ends on Friday mornings. The bus returned in the afternoon when, no doubt, the horse struggled through Ellar Ghyll with the weight of ten or twelve passengers and their shopping.

Some readers will recall the B & B (Blythe & Berwick) bus service into the village which started, I think, in the late twenties. The buses turned round at Lane Ends and picked up passengers at various points in Main Street out to the Hare & Hounds. They left the village at ten-past the hour to Bradford and a quarter-to to Harrogate with (and I write this slowly for the benefit of today's long suffering bus travellers) unfailing regularity! The nine-ten pm to Bradford carried a Royal Mail posting box.

Two early drivers were Tom Kent and Arnold Maltby – as well known as the postmen and milkmen.

Sometime later two popular conductors, who became man and wife, were Clifford Perkins and Annie Fillingham.

Motor transport, as in most areas, has been a major factor in environmental change. Crossing Main Street at peak times today is a hazard and most roads and streets are lined with parked cars.

Looking back, the late Clifford Stradling told me of the time he remembered when there were only three car owners in the village. His uncle Albert Waite (Station Garage), Dr. Hyslop and Frank Wigglesworth (Wigglesworth Clutch Works, Shipley).

There were a few more cars in my youth (Jossie Pearson Craven woke everybody up in a morning with his noisy sports car) but it was always possible to play cricket in Main Street with, perhaps, only the half hour

B & B bus to worry about. Cricket and football were played in front of St. John's Church with choirboys before their practice on Thursday evenings.

There were other instances of traffic scarcity in the thirties. Maggie Hardie, a lady who lived in Walker Road (off Derry Hill) with her brother Bill, shopped at the Co-op. She always walked in the middle of Main Street completely oblivious of the occasional traffic.

Ken Settle reminds me of sledging at break neck speed down Derry Hill to Lane Ends.

Amos Edmondson, a young mechanical genius designed a bogey (basically four pram wheels and a board) which carried four or five passengers (who were brave enough) at high speed from the top of Derry Hill, through the village at Lane Ends and down station fields.

Some readers of my generation may remember, as children, whips and tops and playing marbles or 'taws' in the gutter on the way to school.

Another diversion on the quiet roads was running with hoops – iron ones for boys with a metal hooked rod, and wooden ones for girls which they 'bowled' along with a stick.

Mr and Mrs Albert Waite on Station Road. Mr Waite was one of the first three Menstonians to own a motor car.

The Railway

Below is the poster announcing the opening of Menston Junction Station on 1st March 1873 prior to the building of the present station in 1875. Up to this time – from 1865, when the railway came to Wharfedale – Menston passengers had to board the trains at Guiseley.

This temporary platform was at the junction of the now defunct line to Otley near a signal box and was reached by scrambling down the bank beside the bridge near Well House (now removed), a somewhat undignified manoeuvre for both well dressed business men and their ladies.

MIDLAND RAILWAY.

OPENING OF

MENSTON STATION,

OTLEY & ILKLEY BRANCH.

On SATURDAY, MARCH 1st,

A Station will be opened at MENSTON JUNCTION, and from that date until further notice. Trains will call there as under:---

UP TRAINS.

STATIONS.		WEEKDAYS.			
		a.m.	a.m.	p.m.	p.m.
ILKLEY	dep.	8.20	11.20	3.15	7. 5
Ben Rhydding	,,	8.23	11.24	3.19	7. 9
Burley	,,	8.29	11.31	3.26	7.16
OTLEY	,,	8.27	11.30	3.25	7.15
Menston		8.32	11.35	3.30	7.20
Guiseley	arr.	8.41	11.45	3.40	7.31
Apperley	,,	....	12. 1	3.55	7.47
Bradford...........	,,	9. 8	12.20	4.13	8. 5
LEEDS	,,	9. 8	12.20	4.15	8.23

DOWN TRAINS.

		a.m.	p.m.	p.m.	p.m,	p.m.
LEEDS	dep.	9.45	1.35	4.45	5.45	6.30
Bradford	,,	9.45	1.35	4.50	5.55	6.45
Apperley	,,	10. 7	1.54	....	6. 6	7. 5
Guiseley	,,	10.23	2.13	5.18	6.24	7.25
Menston		10.28	2.20	5.25	6.29	7.30
OTLEY	arr.	10.35	2.25	5.30	6.37	7.37
Burley	,,	10,33	....	....	6.34	7.34
Ben Rhydding .	,,	10.38	..	..	..	7.39
ILKLEY	,,	10.45	....	....	6.45	7.45

Derby, Feb. 24th, 1873. JAMES ALLPORT, General-Manager.

BEMROSE AND SONS, PRINTERS, LONDON AND DERBY

Opening of Menston junction station 1873.

Menston Station in the 1920's.

The Railway was soon to be involved in the expansion of the village and businessmen utilized the new station for their daily journey to Bradford and Leeds.

The 8.33 to Bradford was very popular and the local newsagent provided a profitable service with morning papers.

On the occasion of his marriage in 1880, the Station Master – Mr John Bates was presented with a handsome timepiece, a pair of bronze ornaments – richly designed and an illuminated address by the regular passengers as a mark of appreciation of his civility and attention to their requirements.

The twenties and thirties introduced cheap rail excursions, and evening trips to the coasts and Carlisle were on offer, and were extremely popular.

In 1938 the *Wharfedale Observer* reported that for the second year in succession Menston Station won the Quota Shield for the best percentage increase in passenger traffic for the whole of the LMS transport system.

There was an increase of thirty per cent following twenty-four per cent the previous year. The award was received by the Station Master, Mr W Lee.

Steam trains were replaced by Diesels in 1959 but in 1963, following the Beeching Report, closure notices appeared and all the stations in Wharfedale were threatened.

Commuters from Menston, Guiseley, Burley, Ben Rhydding and Ilkley formed the Ilkley Railway Supporters Association to raise objections. Success was achieved when, in 1972, it was announced that the Leeds to Ilkley line had been reprieved. Eventually the service to Bradford was restored.

Menston Station became unmanned at 5.30 pm on 5th October 1968. On Monday 7th it became a Halt for setting down and picking up passengers – along with Guiseley, Burley and Ben Rhydding. The friendly porter was replaced by an impersonal public address system.

In the early sixties there was another Railway employee who earned passenger appreciation. He was porter John Cooke who lived at Addingham. John left his home at 5.30 am, cycled to Ilkley and came to Menston on the first train. He brought home grown flowers to deck the window sills of the down train waiting room. In winter, there was always a cheery fire and his own transistor radio provided 'music while you wait'.

Our two signal box photographs show the original construction (page 90) which was replaced in 1895 by the much smaller building (above). Incidentally, the bridge was removed when the line was electrified in 1993.

Tram and Trackless

As early as 1902, Menston was included with Ilkley, Burley, Denton and Otley in a suggested Tramway Scheme to be connected with Keighley and East and West Morton and to be known as the Wharfe Valley Tramway Scheme.

However, the idea was soon thought to be too ambitious, involving too many road widenings and diversions and, mercifully, disbanded.

Trams (on rails) ran from Leeds in 1909, first, to the junctions of Green Lane and Apperley Lane at Rawdon. Then, on the 30th June that year, the line reached Station Hotel Guiseley and finally, a short time later, to White Cross. Incidentally, the single fare from Leeds to Guiseley was 3d (old pence).

The double decked trams and later the single decked trackless were housed and maintained in the existing, solid stone building at White Cross now occupied by Nuffied Health Club.

My most pleasant memories of a tram was a ride on the top deck with an open front as it clanked and swayed between frequent stops to Kirkstall Lane or one that took us from Tyrell Street, in Bradford, to Cricket and Football matches at Park Avenue.

I recall there was always a box of sand under a seat downstairs in case of passenger sickness.

In 1910 Leeds Corporation sought permission from the Local Councils of Burley, Menston, Otley and Ilkley to extend the system with trackless trams from White Cross.

Otley agreed in principle but found the cost prohibitive. This led to an application to Parliament by a London syndicate to finance an extension to the system – it was felt that Wharfedale people would welcome the proposal.

Strong objections came, however, from sections of both Menston and Burley Councils and no support at all came from Ilkley.

Trackless trams were described as 'the worst abomination on the highway' by Mr Charles Tankard of Menston Parish Council 'The trams' he said 'ripped up the roads and splashed people as they passed on wet days'. Councillor F D Moore of Burley said 'I do not think there is the slightest necessity for trams – they will be a perfect nuisance. The village is pestered enough with motor cars'. (The speed limit through Burley at this time was ten m.p.h.).

FARES.

GUISELEY AND OTLEY AND BURLEY.

GUISELEY (White Cross) and OTLEY.

"White Cross" and Gill Mill	1d.
"Hare & Hounds" and Kineholm	1d.
Gill Mill and Westbourne	1d.
Kineholm and Maypole (Otley)	1d.
Through fare between Oxford Rd., Guiseley, and Otley by change of car at White Cross	3d.

GUISELEY (White Cross) and BURLEY.

"White Cross" and Post No. 8	1d.
"Hare & Hounds" and Railway Bridge	1d.
Post No. 8 and Junction of Otley Road, Burley	1d.
Railway Bridge and Station Road, Burley	1d.
Through fare between Oxford Rd., Guiseley, and Burley by change of car at White Cross	3d.

SPECIAL FARES.

PASSENGERS JOINING CARS BEFORE 7.45 a.m.:—

Any Two consecutive Ordinary penny Stages on the same car	1d.
Any Three " " " " "	1½d.

and so on.

A Ticket available for the Return Journey over the same section of route by a through car after 12 noon may be purchased at the same time at above rates.

SPECIAL RETURN FARES:—

Between Oxford Road, Guiseley and Otley by change of car	3d.
Between Oxford Road, Guiseley and Burley by change of car	3d.
Between Otley and Burley by change of car	3d.

CHILDREN'S FARES:—

Children between the age of Five and Twelve (or under 15 if going to or from School) will travel at half fares. No fare will be less than a Half-penny and in the case of a 1½d. or 2½d. adult fare the charge will be 1d. and 1½d. respectively and so on.

PASSENGERS' GOODS or LUGGAGE.

(CARRIED AT OWNERS' RISK ONLY.)

Personal Luggage, such as Portmanteaus, Trunks, and Suit Cases, up to 28 lbs., and Workmen's Tools will be carried FREE.

Above 28 lbs. Personal Luggage will be charged same rate as Goods or Luggage not personal.

Small Articles up to 14 lbs.	FREE.
Exceeding 14 lbs. and under 42 lbs.	1d.
Exceeding 42 lbs. and under 60 lbs.	2d.

Luggage exceeding 60 lbs. in weight will not be carried.

August, 1915.

BY ORDER.

Trackless Fares Guide from 1915.

Ilkley observed 'with trackless trams, the advent of the cheap tripper is made more probable and Ilkley wisely realizes that its future welfare might he endangered by such an invasion'.

In spite of objections, the scheme was finally approved by Otley, Burley, Wharfedale Rural and Menston Councils and, in 1915 the opening of the new route from White Cross Guiseley to Otley took place. The first 'trackless' was welcomed with due ceremony by Mr Harold Duncan, Chairman of Otley Council.

The mile and a half from the Fox and Hounds to Burley was completed shortly after.

The trackless service ceased in 1928 or 9 and the trams came to a halt in 1934. Both were replaced by the motor bus.

My memory of the trackless was that it was yellow and the contribution it invariably made to the bustle and excitement on a Whit Monday morning when, it seemed, all Menston assembled on the Main Road to see Bradford *Telegraph & Argus* annual walk.

Cattle, going to Otley Market and walkers added to the traffic congestion and frequently a trolley boom became disconnected from the overhead wires – much to the amusement of the crowd and the consternation of the conductor who had to use a long bamboo pole to reconnect it.

The Cornmill

One of Menston's oldest landmarks before it was demolished to make way for the present Cornmill Flats in Bradford Road, built between 1968-71. The Mill was of unknown antiquity and belonged to the owners of Menston Hall. Wheat, maize, barley and rye were brought for grinding by local farmers.

The Cornmill before demolition in the 1960's.

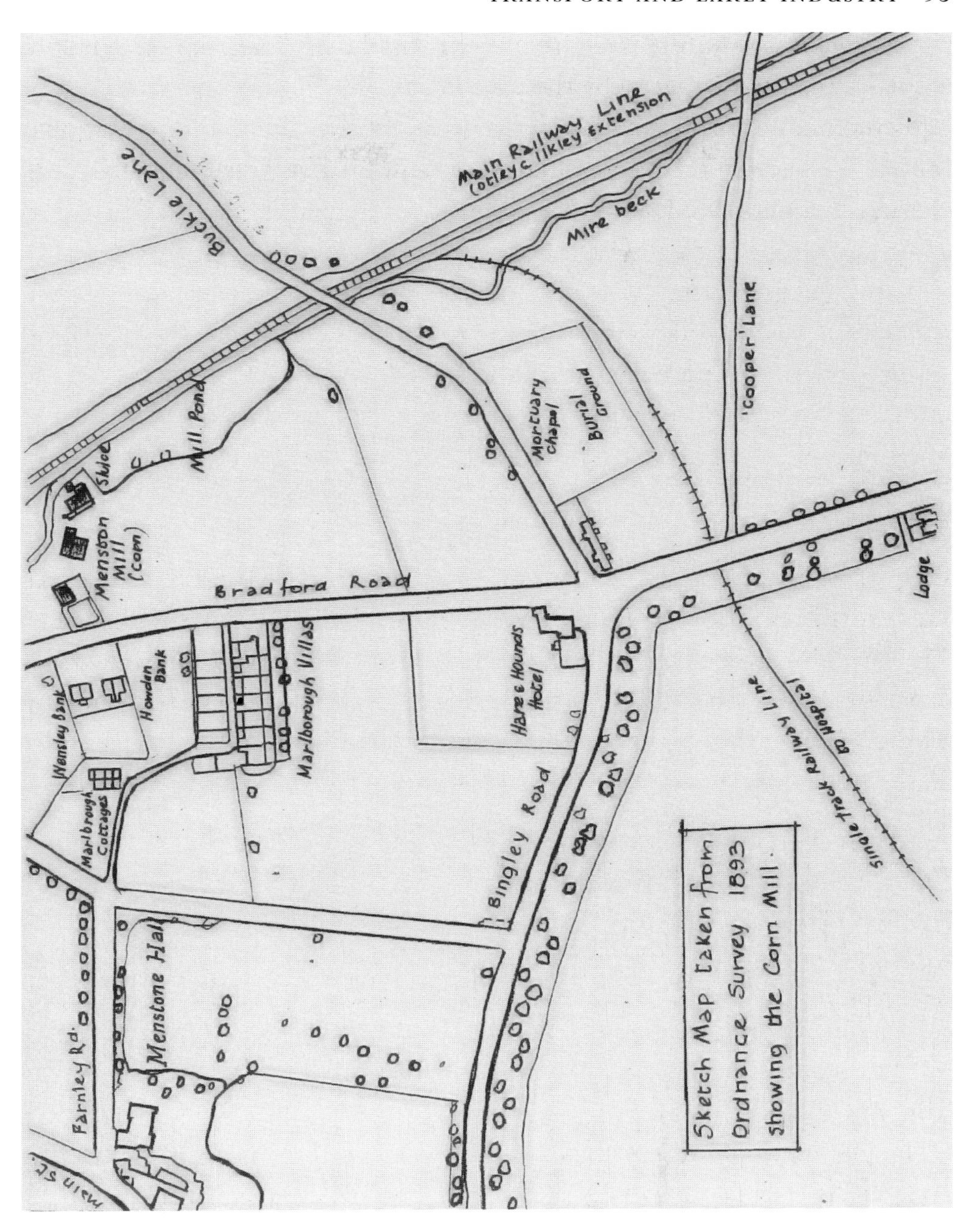

Sketch map taken from ordnance survey 1893
showing the Cornmill.

It closed as a mill in 1907 when the water supply dried up. The last millers were the Claphams who moved to Burley besides the Wharfe.

A sale conducted by Messrs Dacres in 1876 offered the mill (part of the settled estate of the Fawkes family), with the Reservoir, thirty-six feet diameter water wheel and drying kiln.

Feeding the mill dam was Tranmere Beck which starts on the Odda at Hawksworth. It becomes two streams in the fields at Highroyds Hospital.

One stream continues to the Mill Beck under the Main Road near White Cross, behind St. Mary's School, under Buckle Lane to the Dam, thence to Ellar Ghyll and the River Wharfe. The other stream ran into Guiseley. The Dam, now overgrown, had to be remade when the Railway was constructed in 1865, the cost being borne by the Railway Company.

After the Claphams left, the premises were occupied by several farmers Thackray, Hardaker and Pratt (the last resident). They were also used at one time by a Woodworker named Porritt.

The owner of the Cornmill at the time of its demolition was apparently a Mr A F Greene of Shipley who presented the seven millstones to Otley Museum some of which are still to be seen in Otley's Wharfe Meadows.

Rombalds Moor Bleach Works and 19th century Mills in the Glen

Miss Fletcher and Mr Laurence both briefly discuss the mills in the Glen at Woodhead and regard the Bleach Mill as being more concerned with Menston than either Woodhead or Burley, mainly because the access was from Menston.

The majority of workers came from Menston and the first village cricket team in 1880 was composed largely from employees of the mill. Members included James McKinley (the Manager) and old Menston names – Weightman, White, Cole and Hancock.

The origin of the works is uncertain – it is believed to have been a woollen mill and possibly owned by James Padgett who later lived at Menston Low Hall.

Bleach Mill, Menston.

In 1870 the mill was bought by Joseph Gill & Sons, linen bleachers. They constructed the present Bleach Mill Lane and, in 1890, employed about forty people, including some women. Thirty horses were kept near Low Fold behind Hagwood Farm.

Yarns were bleached and later woven rags for paper making. When the mill closed in 1927, tarpaulins were being bleached and one reason for closure was because of excess pollution flowing down the Dry Beck to the River Wharfe at Burley.

The mill chimney was dismantled brick by brick and the only buildings which remain are the manager's house (now occupied by Mr Simon Richmond), the adjacent pay office, joiner's shop and stables.

Turning left from the footpath, beyond Bleach Mill, is the Glen now a local, beauty spot and a delightful walk – in dry weather.

Halfway up was the Middle or Hargreaves Mill. This was a spinning and scribbling mill powered by water from a dam on Carr Beck on which, in my youth, was a homemade raft affording hours of pleasure during the school holidays.

A report in the *Wharfedale Observer* 1891 records a party held on the ice of Messrs. Hargreaves' dam, 'a pretty scene lighted by thirty coloured Chinese lanterns'.

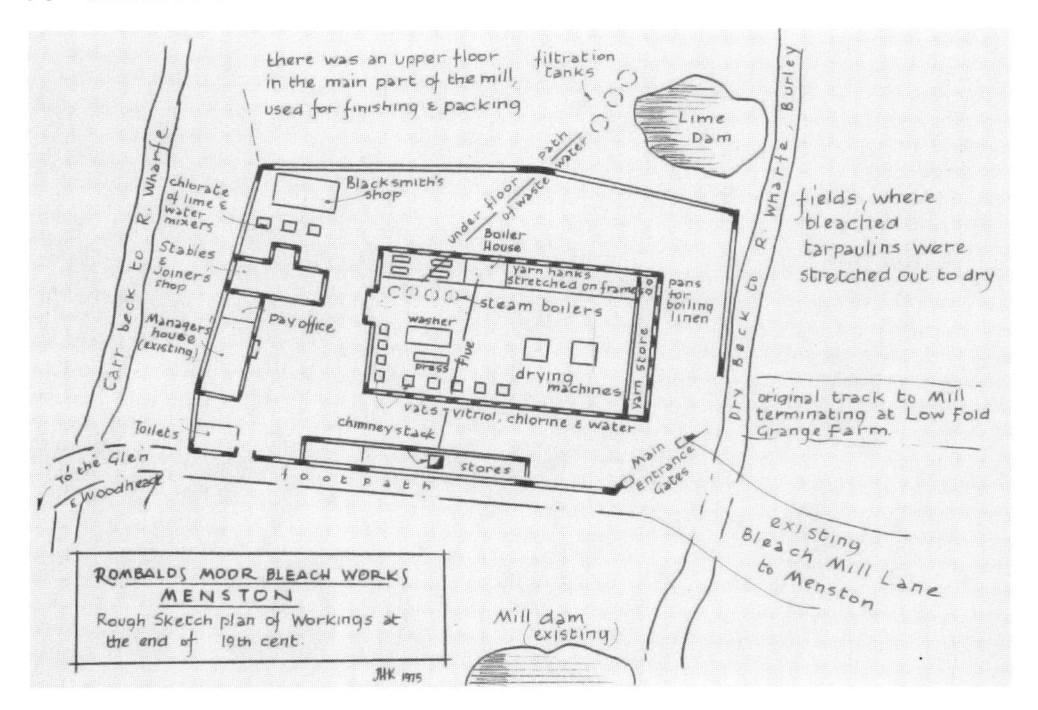

Rough plan of 19th century mills in the Glen and Green Lane Menston and Woodhead.

The Mill, which in 1819 was owned by J Baldwin had a cast iron water wheel, one of the largest in the district.

A steam engine was also used to supplement the water power.

All that remains of the mill is the chimney and part of the dam sluice gates.

Myrtle Grove Mill was on the site of the two existing cottages and its water supply came from a dam in Green Lane higher up the Glen. This mill was also for spinning and scribbling. Owners at one time were Corless and Padgett and. in 1839, William Demain.

The substantial dwellings on the left going up were at various times mill workers' cottages and workshops.

Mr John Brear, a member of a local history group under Mrs Margaret Warwick, has established that there was another mill in the Glen-Listers and the owner in 1819 was Nathan Hustler.

Crossing the Woodhead Road into Green Lane was a spinning mill in the early nineteenth century, to the west of Turnpike House. It is clearly

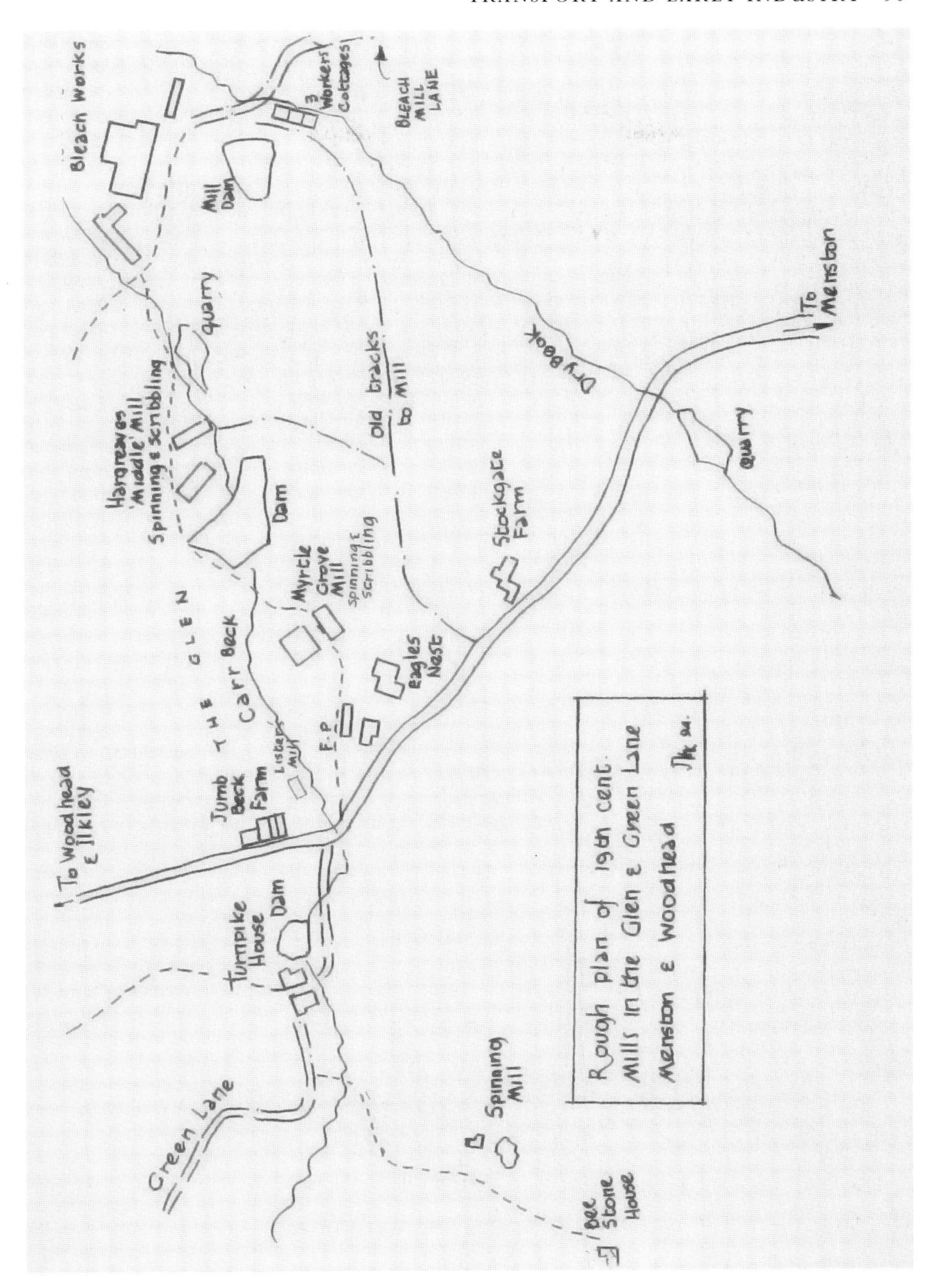

Rough plan of 19th century mills in the Glen and Green Lane Menston and Woodhead.

The only remaining buildings of Bleach Mill – the manager's house, offices and stables.

marked, together with the mill dam, on the first six inch ordnance survey map of the area, the survey for which was made in 1847. The last owner was William Bridges.

The Mills in Ellar Ghyll

On the 1847 six inch map this area is referred to as Hell Hole Gill and there are shown four mills.

On the west side of the present road is Gill Mill or, as it was known, Hargreaves Bobbin Mill.

Opposite, in the Ghyll, is marked Mill (spinning) on the site of which I believe is the existing Murphy Engineering Works. This mill was owned at one time by Moons of Guiseley and Wildmans of Menston.

Further down was the New Mill (scribbling). The chimney for this mill in living memory was on the opposite side of the road.

The mill at the extreme end of the Ghyll, towards Otley, was Low Mill or Derry Diddle Mill (wool spinning and scribbling).

These mills all had dams, weirs and water wheels and, according to Gladys Baker, work was carried on in candle light when daylight failed.

Reference to the Bobbin Mill is made by Edward Lee writing in 1862.

'There were no Trade Union rules at this time and I remember five of us getting 3s-6d (17½ p) each a week for making small bobbins for worsted'.

Mr Lee also makes an interesting reference to Jonathan Peate, a founder of Nunroyd Mills, Guiseley in 1868 who owned the Bobbin Mill.

'Jonathan Peate was a young man passing up and down Menston from Burley Woodhead to Ellar Ghyll. He had no transport and wore a long chequered brat (coat) and at this time lived with his parents in the top cottage of the two still standing in Ellar Ghyll'.

It is possible, I think, that Peates and Moons would have built their mills in Menston rather than Guiseley had not Ayscough Fawkes decreed that there should be no industry on the Menston Estate.

Chimney, Middle Mill, The Glen.

When the mills closed with the Industrial Revolution and the works were transferred to Guiseley, the Ghyll was eventually taken over by George Butler for a scrap metal yard. Some buildings were converted into warehouses, one having three storey's with road access to each level.

Notes Re Menston Water Works

a Originally constructed 1875 by the Menston Waterworks Co.
b Bought by Wharfedale Rural District Council 1900
c Transferred to Ilkley UDC in 1937 as a result of revised boundaries
d Transferred to Rombalds Water Board in 1962. Now Yorkshire Water.

Sources of Supply

a Gathering grounds 40 acres
b 3 main sources
i. Craven Hall Spring
Wet weather yield 1500 galls/hour.
Dry weather yield 200 galls/hour
a. Bee Stone (main source) located ¼ mile from Filter House Rt of Shooting Range, corner of a field. Wet weather yield 4500 galls/hour Dry weather yield 100 galls/hour
3. The Reservoir Enclosure Short adil (Tunnel) driven into the Millstone Grit formation. Wet weather yield 1400 galls/hour Dry weather yield 700 galls/hour Generally surface water pure and soft.

The Reservoir

When Wharfedale RDC took it over in 1900, the storage capacity was found to be three small tanks with a capacity of 13200 galls not enough for one days supply.

The firm Silcock & Simpson designed and constructed the present reservoir.

197 feet x 87 feet x 16 feet 3 inches deep capacity 1,750,000 gallons, equaling sixty days supply based on a population of 1,500 people at twenty galls/day/head.

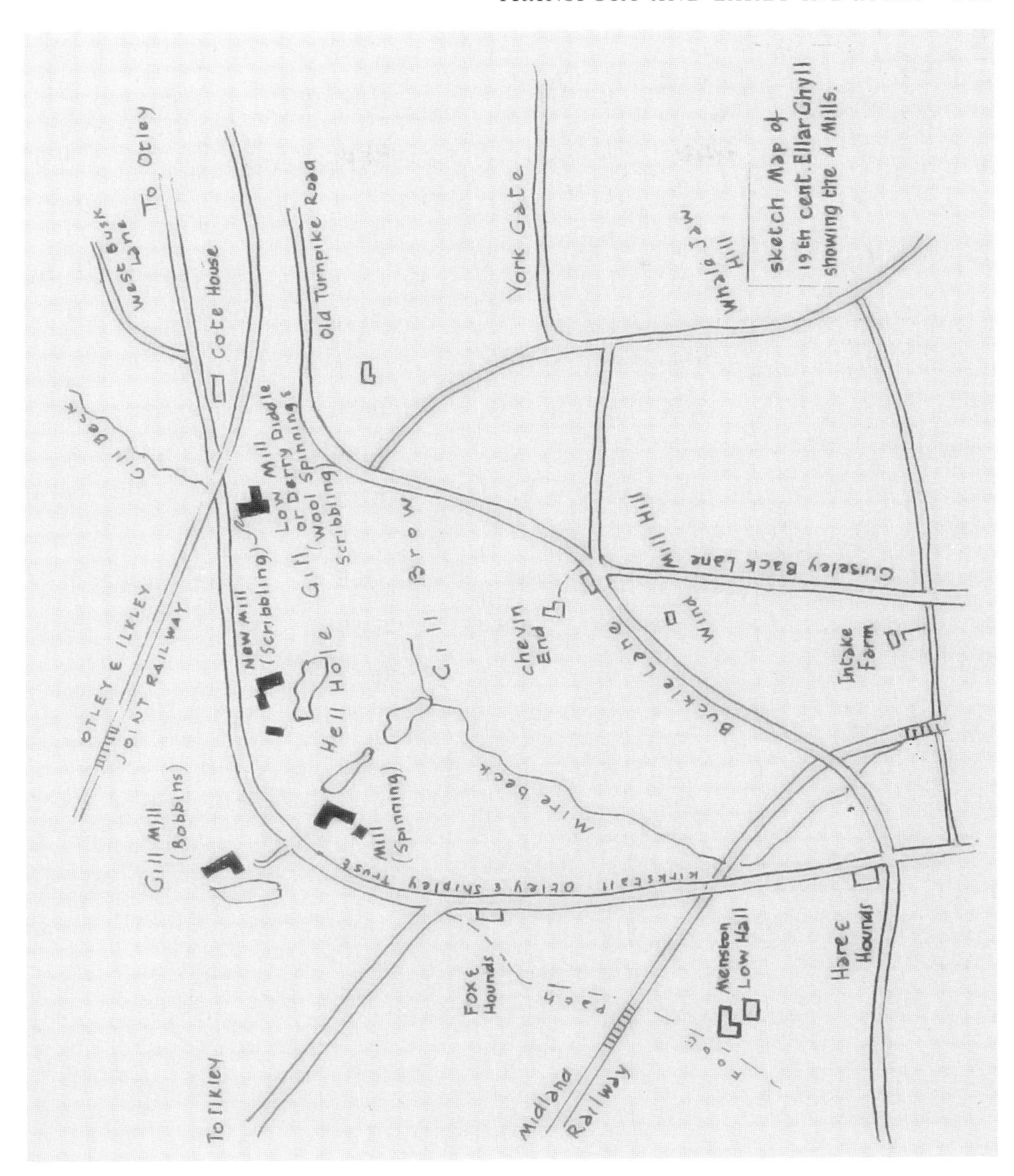

Sketch map of 19th century Ellar Ghyll showing the four mills.

Distribution

System of Mains. One main direct to Menston Village via Moor Lane – along Main Street where it joined the second main which came down Occupation Lane and Bingley Road. There were other subsidiary mains spreading from these main trunk mains.

A standpipe in Occupation Lane diverted excess water into the Reservoir from the second main if the village drawing power was small.

Filter House Feb 1923 Mr W B Richardson, Clarence Drive. Bradford City analyst, took a sample of water from his tap and found it to be Plumbo-Solvent – his findings caused Wharfedale RDC to install filters, a Battery of three containing sand with a top layer of Magnisite to filter and correct the acidity.

After twenty-five years, the storage was found to be inadequate. The engineers failed to visualise the growth of Menston – twenty galls/head/day was too low in view of the advance of sanitation.

HOSPITALS AND WARTIME

Menston Asylum before changes to the clock tower.

High Royds Hospital in the 1980's.

High Royds Hospital

The hospital, designed for the treatment of mental disorders, was opened in October, 1888. Taking three years to build, it was originally named the West Riding Pauper Lunatic Asylum and the 300 acre site at Menston Moor bottom was purchased from Ayscough Fawkes for £18,000. The overall cost was in the region of £250,000 and, initially, accommodation was for 800 patients.

Patients and staff virtually doubled Menston's population and, with the opening of the Railway Station, the Asylum was a factor in the rapid growth of the village.

The name was changed to Menston Mental Hospital in 1923 and to High Royds Hospital in 1963. Through the years there were several 'tags' given to the institution. Asylum became 'sylum', 'up there', 'up yonder' or, to outsiders, simply 'Menston'. Even today, in some circumstances, one can still get some funny looks if one admits to coming from Menston!

The first Medical Superintendent, Dr J G McDowall, whose annual salary was £400, was a member of Menston's first Parish Council in 1894 and, although closely connected to the village, the hospital was very much a self-sufficient community.

It had its own farms, Thorpe, Odda and Norcroft under a Farm Bailiff. Market gardens produced much of its required food. Almost every trade establishment was on site and a railway was connected to the main line. The branch railway carrying bulky supplies to the hospital ran right up to 1951 and the late Eric Rogers was the authority on its history.

The branch started from the down line of the Midland Railway at a point between Cooper Lane and Buckle Lane bridges. There was a siding to which trucks from Guiseley would be shunted. Movements would be monitored by the Guiseley and Menston signal boxes. The line passed through a short cutting and under the Bradford Road through a small tunnel which still exists.

The first loco was a small steam tank engine but, after some time, it was realised the gradient was too steep, especially in bad weather. In the early 1890s the line was electrified and a small electric loco was purchased. The loco carrying two men, one to drive, the other a trolley man who also operated the levers which moved the points.

In 1924 the loco was replaced by a modern electric hauling unit manufactured by the English Electric Co.

In the middle of the 1930s the Railway Company, later LMS, insisted on repairs to the sidings which would cost £400. The Hospital Board decided the amount could not be justified as, by now, most of the hospital supplies were being brought by road. So, the loco and line were mothballed.

The line was brought back into use during the Second World War, but, as petrol and diesel supplies were restored, it was used less and less. Finally, in 1951, closure came when everything was dismantled and sold for scrap.

The longest serving Medical Superintendent was Dr Sam Edgerley (1906-1933) and, as one would expect, the community produced a wealth of characters and personalities from both patients and staff.

The various departments were staffed in many instances by the patients (under supervision), as a form of occupational therapy.

My father, George Kell, was the hospital's butcher. Four or five patients assisted him in supplying meat to inmates, the numbers of which peaked at 2,400 in 1944.

Two of his 'staff' deserve a mention. Cecil was an intellectual and a former master at a Grammar School. He wrote poetry and, as a mathematician, he applied Calculus (Maxima and Minima) to reduce the amount of metal foil required in a corned beef tin, whilst maintaining the same volume of meat. Cecil also made wine and his own brand of rye whisky.

Foster was a permanent hospital resident and a big, powerful man. He effectively applied the pole-axe in the slaughterhouse.

It was Foster's job at cricket matches to raise and lower the Union Jack which fluttered over the pavilion.

Nurses were given two weeks holiday a year, to be taken between January 1st and December 31st. Walker Brearly took his annual leave during the first two weeks of January, would you believe, just in case he died and 'missed out'!

Male nurses, or attendants, whose duties were mainly custodial, were not always asked for nursing qualifications, but rather how good they were at cricket, football, singing, acting or playing an instrument. This was because the staff was expected to entertain the patients.

The hospital had its own orchestra, playing for the regular Friday night dances and music for other social occasions.

The cricket team with the best of grounds and facilities could match any team in the area. Perhaps there were as many as 200 patients brought from the wards on a Saturday afternoon to watch the cricket, until teatime.

The Centenary of the hospital was duly celebrated in 1988 and Dr Roy Hullins produced a booklet outlining its history. Some interesting facts to emerge from the book: Nearly 3000 people lie buried in unmarked graves in an area in Buckle Lane near the ambulance station and nearly another 1000 are buried in pauper graves in Guiseley Cemetery.

Records show that, in the early days, a normal working week for nurses was eighty-seven hours and the average cost of each patient to the ratepayers was 9 shillings or less than 50p a week.

TRIBUTE ON THE DEATH OF EARL LLOYD GEORGE

As fades a flower in some woodland dell,
That feels no more the heat of summer sun,
So ceased to breath again the noble mind,
Who's days have numbered and who's race is run,
Ask not of me the doughty deeds of fame,
The crowning glory to an ancient name,
In happier days shall grateful kindred find,
He served his country and he loved his kind.

G.C. Bergan (patient) 1945.

Norcroft Farm by J. H. Kell.

Odda Farm by J. H. Kell.

High Rhodes now High Royds Hall.

High Rhodes

Now called the High Royds Hall is on hospital land between Menston and Hawksworth.

The history of this mid-seventeenth century house and its occupants, mainly the Rhodes family, has been thoroughly documented by Alastair Laurence.

When Ayscough Fawkes sold 287 acres of farmland in 1882 to the West Riding County Council on which to build Menston Asylum, the house was split into three cottages for hospital farmers and their families.

Now, as a protected (or listed) building, the house has been restored as a single dwelling, retaining its age old character and charm. The splendid view from its windows towards the Odda and Hawksworth remains much as it did three hundred years ago, as yet unspoilt.

A successful hospital football team 1927-8.

Left to Right – *Back row:* Harry Coultas (referee), Georg Blackburn, Eddie Brown, Jack Robson, ---- Thompson, Gordon Lamb, Harry Wormersley, Myles Hayley, George Kell, Lister Mann. ***Middle row:*** Harry Mckinley, Doctor Edgerley, Jack Sutton (Captain), Mr Sampson (Chief-Attendant), ---- Goldthorp. ***Front row***: Bob Vernon and Jim Shaw.

Wharfedale Children's Hospital

In January, 1988, Environment Minister, Nicholas Ridley, announced that he had approved plans to develop the site of the Wharfedale Children's Hospital – closed by the Ministry of Health in 1985, and to uphold the decision of an enquiry, lasting 10 days, to preserve Green Belt land between Derry Hill and Moor Lane. An application had been made to build 100 houses on this site and construct a bus turning circle at the bottom of Moor Lane near to the Mount Pleasant cottages.

Wharfedale Isolation Hospital Menston.

For three years the Menston Community Association, ably led by their Chairman, David Llewellyn, vigorously opposed the development of both sites.

The hospital, the site of which covered an area of over twelve acres between Otley and Burley Roads, was built in 1904 and was first developed by the Wharfedale Union Joint Isolation Hospital. There were seven separate buildings including pavilions for typhoid fever and scarlet fever. There were forty-six beds for the treatment of patients from Otley, Ilkley, Aireborough, Horsforth, Baildon and Wharfedale Rural District areas. The approximate overall cost, including the site, was £17,000.

Menston Councillors actively involved in the undertaking were Joseph Crowther and Ben Shaw. Dr. J W Hyslop was the Medical Officer for many years.

Extensions were made in 1933 and, in 1948, the hospital became part of Ilkley and Otley Hospitals run by a Hospital Management Committee under the Leeds Regional Hospital Board.

In 1949 Otley Council approved the conversion of the Joint Isolation Hospital to a primarily long stay children's hospital and, as such, it functioned for over thirty years.

Most of the children returned to their homes at weekends and during normal school holidays.

In the early eighties policy changed and the authorities decided to make 'greater efforts to get these children out of such hospitals and to have as normal a home and school life as possible'!

The Minister of Health, Mr Barney Heyhoe, was assured that 'better and more suitable care was available elsewhere' and he made the decision to close in 1985.

The hospital was sold to Higgs & Hill, a London based firm of developers for £4.5million in 1986. Planning application for redevelopment of the site was granted in 1989 but the building of Ellar Gardens did not commence until 1993.

During excavations, in preparation for building, local archaeologists discovered a section of the Roman Road – which ran from York to Ribchester in Lancashire.

I have a vague recollection of a hospital existing for a short time on the Chevin, dealing with infectious diseases.

Menston's War Memorials

The name of those villagers who fell in the First World War (1914-1918) is recorded in St. John's Parish and Methodist Churches.

The Memorial is a bungalow in Park Road originally occupied by District Nurse Craven, a well known and lovable village personality for many years.

At the end of the Second World War (1939-1945), from the money generously subscribed by villagers, a Memorial Committee decided on three objects.

1. A stained glass memorial window in the Methodist Church.
2. An oak cabinet and processional cross in St. John's Church.

In each church would be a Book of Remembrance, a record of all who had served in HM Forces and a plaque recording the names of those who died.

3. A Garden of Remembrance.

The bungalow in Park Road serving as a memorial to those men of the village who died in the First World War (1914-1918).

The first two objects were immediately achieved but item 3 caused a problem, due to 'lamentable delays' and non-availability of a suitable site. It was fifteen years before a Committee, chaired by Mr Eric Busby, proposed a sunken garden in front of Kirklands!

In order to construct the garden it meant the fine old chestnut trees should be felled and replaced by flowering cherry.

The scheme caused such a furore, with a majority of villagers against chopping the trees down, that it was scrapped in favour of a site in the corner of Menston Hall grounds.

The Memorial Garden, opened by Mr Busby in 1962, featured a covered colonnade as a shelter supported by stone pillars and containing seats and a plaque bearing the sixteen names of the village fallen.

For a short time the Garden fulfilled its purpose as a place of quiet solitude, particularly for the older generation.

Eventually, however, the shelter became misused and vandalised by groups of motorcyclists and gangs of young people who gathered there. The heavy wooden seats were broken and torn from their mountings and, generally, the whole area lost its meaning as a memorial. It became a public disgrace and an 'eyesore'!

The memorial plaque, erected in 2008 to the memory of 50 Menston and Woodhead men killed in the First World War (1914-1918).

The covered colonnade in the memorial garden, opened in 1962, in memory of the 16 villagers who fell in the Second World War (1939-1945).

Perhaps sometime in the future, when they are older and wiser, the individuals responsible may come to regret their mindless behaviour.

The Ilkley Parish Council, particularly Councillor Peter Williams, did consider ways and means to retain the memorial but, in 1984, decided, by a nine to one majority, with four abstentions, it should be demolished.

The plaque was resited on a piece of rock (I believe from Ilkley Moor) outside Kirklands.

For several years, a Menston resident, Mrs Judith Knaggs felt that there was some injustice in not fully recognizing the sacrifice that 50 Menston and Woodhead men had made during the First World War (1914-1918).

Mrs Knaggs, supported by Councilor Dale Smith, was the instigator of a campaign to raise money towards the cost of a new memorial.

This was successful and a plaque, mounted on a stone plinth, with the names of the fallen was dedicated by local clergy, at a service in front of Kirklands on 11th November 2008.

In 1947 in a Bill Bowes benefit match played at the Fox, a team of 1914-18 war veterans beat an eleven selected from 1939-45 ex-servicemen.

The memorial plaque dedicated to the memory of the 16 men who gave their lives in the Second World War (1939-1945).

A Christmas card sent from Menston to forces in Second World War.
The church hall and B & B bus with left to right, Mr A S Maston (headmaster), Mr Henry Hargrave, Mrs Bobby Wigglesworth and Mrs Jack Walker.

The 1914-18 XI. **Left to right** – ***Back row:*** Norman Patterson, John Ellicott, Syd Sunderland, Edgar Rawnsley, George Kell, G.V. Mackrell, Wilson Haigh (umpire). ***Seated***: Eddie Walker, Norman Hancock, Billy Rogers Arthur Shaw, Bob Weightman.

The 1939-45 XI. **Left to right** – ***Back row***: Harold Bellerby, Wilfred Speak, Jim Riggott, Fred Brooking, Donald Hancock, Dick Hargrave, Arthur Bearpark, Henry Hargrave (umpire). ***Seated***: Arnold Kempton, Eddie Jefferson, Ronnie Dyson, Leslie Glaister.

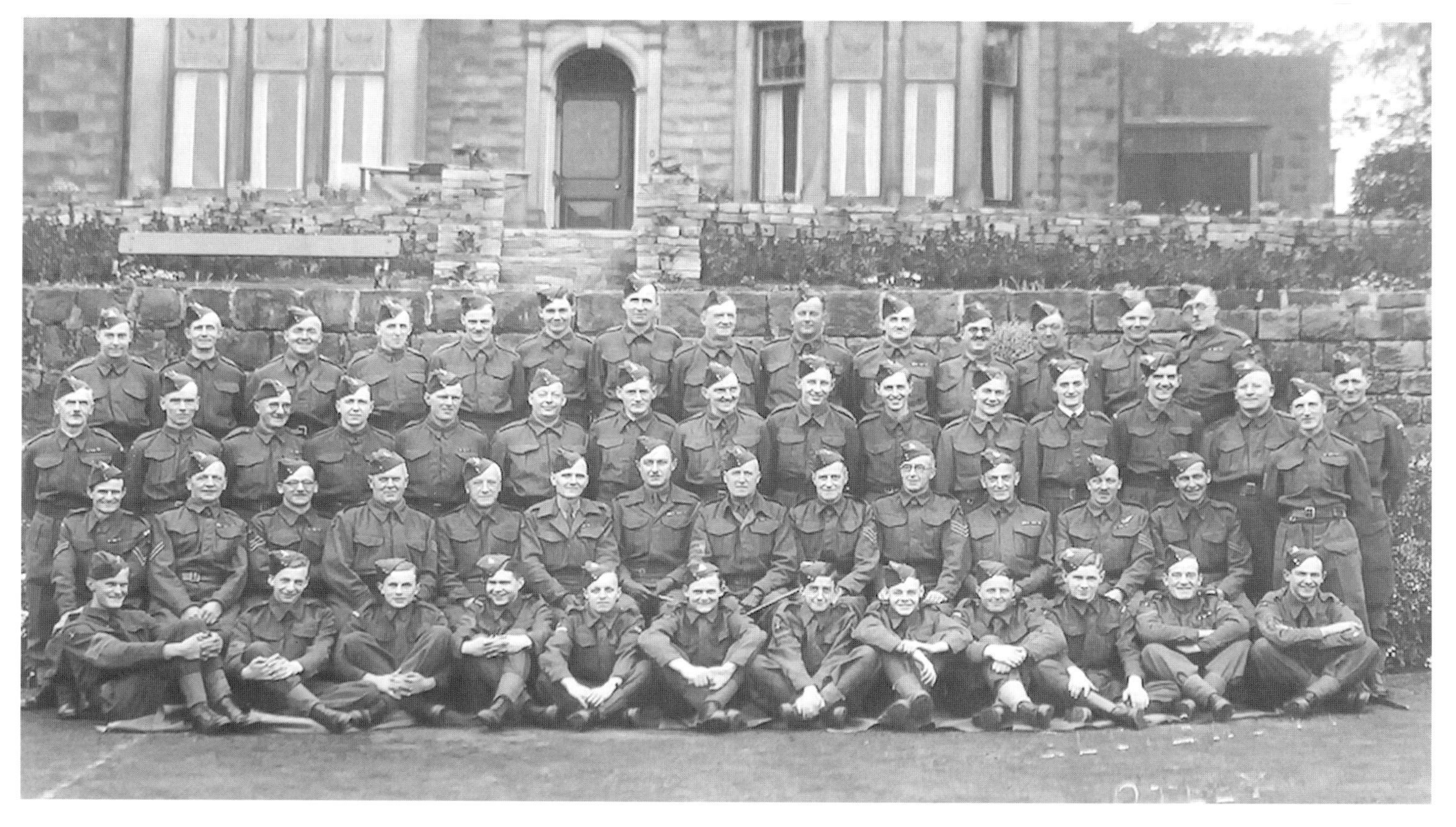

Menston's Home Guard at Beech house, Cleasby Road. **Left to right – *Back row:*** ---, ---, Billy Greetham, ---, Cecil Dingley, Gordon Newton, – Hillas, ---, Jack Sharp, Harry Dumville, J. B. Ickeringill, ---, ---, ---. ***2nd row...*** – Frizell, W. Lee, ---, ---, Stan Birrell, Ben Tillotson, ---, Jack Heron, Teddy Weightman, Jeffray Weightman, Donald Hancock, Len Turner, Bob Mumby, Hanson Toothill, Reg Biss, ---. ***3rd row:*** Frank Pickard, Walter Pitts, Harry Pottage, Dick Todd, Charlie Hudson, G. C. Walter, J. O. Seager, W. J. Price, Edgar Oldfield, Bob Close, Frank Barnes, Maurice Adams, ---. ***Front row***: ---, Herbert Hudson, Peter Frizell, Henry Beanland, Alan Coupland, Albert Hancock, Jack Land, ---, Donald Todd, Dennis Lee, ---, Tommy Robertshaw. – Can anyone supply the missing names?

Menston's Special Constables in the grounds of Cadems cafe. Second world war 1939-45. **Left to right**
Back row: --, --, --, Alfred S. Maston, Bert Cooper, Norman Hancock, --, --. ***Middle row***: --, Bill Storr, Edward Hanson, --, Howard White, Bob Weightman, Miles Beaumont, – Fowlet, Fred Ramsden, Douglas Hartley, Leslie Smith.
Front row: W. Berry, --, J. Marjerison, George Robertshaw, Arthur Outersides, Arthur Voigt, Harry Hannam, Henry Hargrave, Fred Willis, Stanley Ryley, Norman Moore.– Can anyone supply the missing names?

DRAMATIC ARTS, MUSIC AND OTHER SOCIETIES

Menston Amateur Dramatics

THE village has a proud record in Amateur Drama extending over a hundred years. Between 1903 and 1928 its first Dramatic Society, apart from the war years, produced a Musical Show almost every year.

There were many Gilbert and Sullivan operas, including the Mikado, which involved a full orchestra and a cast of over sixty.

In the early years, the shows were produced in the Council (Junior) School, and then later, in the twenties, were lavishly staged in the King's Hall, Ilkley.

The late Mrs Jessie Sunderland (nee Richmond) said that many of the cast and audience travelled by train from Menston to Ilkley: 'Those in evening dress looked quite something.'

Old Menston names appearing were: Tankard, Dowson, White, Shepherd, Hyslop, Grieg, Biss, Pickles and Weightman.

My own introduction to the magic of the theatrical stage was in 1934 seeing the newly formed British Legion Players in their first production R C Sheriff's *Journey's End* as I sat, spellbound, on a window sill in the old Church Hall.

Adding authenticity to this war-time classic was an entire cast of ex-servicemen: J O Seager, A S Maston, F Wall, A Outtersides, T V Bilton, J Newton, S Biltcliffe, A Weightman, G Robertshaw and C Bilton. H Leyshon was the producer.

Other memorable performances up to 1939 were; *None but the Brave, The Wrecker, Edgar Wallace's The Case of the Frightened Lady and The Amazing Dr Clitterhouse.*

The Menston Thespians, were formed in the late thirties and, I believe, owe their foundation to a group closely associated with the Menston Sick Nursing Society which existed at this time. Dr. Hyslop was president and the Society's funds benefited from the shows.

In 1938 they presented *The Housemaster* in the Church Hall. William Foster Shepherd produced the play and also took a leading part. During the Second World War, a group containing past and future Thespians, operated as The Menston Dramatic Art Class. They gave several memorable performances including *Dear Octopus, To Kill a Cat, The Linden Tree and When We Are Married*. Bert Cooper, Margaret Wilkinson and Eileen Mitchell were outstanding players. In 1955 the Thespians were reestablished with another performance of Priestley's *When We Are Married*. Two plays were successfully produced almost every year to delighted audiences drawn from the village and much further afield. A pantomime appeared during Christmas periods.

A play *Celebration* was appropriately presented when the group moved from the Church Hall to the new Community Centre at Kirklands in 1973. Leading past players and producers who come to mind are: Jack Pitts, Robert and Betty Driver, Kay Aspinal, Christine Parkinson and Margaret Wilkinson.

Stalwarts include Rae Barker, Joyce Chavener, Frank Marrow, Gordon Whitehead and John Howell who has recently died. Behind the scenes were Barbara Hannam, Peter Finlay and Judy White. Sadly Barbara, who gave such willing service to many village organisations died in 2008.

New bright stars are appearing regularly and, with a healthy list of patrons, it is reasonable to hope Menston Thespians will continue to make their valuable contribution to village life.

Particularly in the twenties and thirties, the Parish Church had its annual Parochial Tea and Concert – usually in January.

Scholars, Staff and Choir contributed with music, songs and sketches to the evening's entertainment. Rev. F. A. Hodd, in his time, always delighted with his own topical verses set to a popular tune of the day for the audiences to join in.

The Methodists, too, always had an eye for homespun entertainment. Ladies and Men's Weekends always produced a play of sorts and, again, Sunday School Scholars and staff were encouraged to take to the stage. In 1958 an enthusiasm for drama led to the formation of a Dramatic Society. Jack Pitts, Elizabeth Woodhead, Margaret Edwards-Smith, Harry and

Margaret Bexon and Robert Normandale were outstanding players. The group disbanded in the late sixties when Jack Pitts transferred his theatrical talents to the Menston Thespians until his untimely death in 1978.

In 1984, as the Church approached its centenary, a Building Fund was launched to extend the entrance vestibule. Perhaps the most ambitious and spectacular event in the cause of the Building Fund was the production of a version of the musical *The Sound of Music* which took place in the Church, in May. From within the church membership Enid Tindall, the producer, brought together a wealth of technical skill and musical talent which delighted Menston's community for three memorable evenings.

During recent years the momentum of the new Drama Group has been maintained. Along with Enid Tindall, the names of Musical Directors Eleanor Cree, Sue Brown, Thelma Price and Michael Pratt must be added in the productions of another eight or nine musical event – filling the Church to capacity.

Long remembered will be *Brigadoon, Anne of Green Gables, Free as Air,* and *My Fair Lady*.

Menston Music and Arts Society

On 1st September 1943, Wilfred Hannam was asked to write to all Menston residents inviting their views on 'providing for ourselves some entertainment or diversions of high quality'.

The response to the circular was such as to inspire the formation of The Menston Music and Arts Society – a very successful venture which ran for about six years.

The Chairman of a seventeen strong committee, formed from 'leading lights' of the village, was George R Lawson, the Secretary was Wilfred Hannam and treasurers were Tom Moorhouse and Andrew Young.

The main object of the Society, which produced a set of 18 Rules, was to 'encourage Music, Art and Literature in Menston'.

Membership was 1/- (5p) and a season ticket (admitting to all events) £1. The first season's membership numbered 364 of whom 187 were season ticket holders.

What a galaxy of stars, in their own field, came to our village during those six years. They included Artist Adrian Hill; Singers Isobel Baillie, Doris Gambell and Kathleen Ferrier; Pianists Denis Mathews, Gerald Moore and Menston's Erik Brewerton, Albert Sammons (Violin), Leon Goossens (Oboe) and lectures by Bernard Newman, Phyllis Bentley and Beatrice Forbes Robertson.

There were exhibitions of paintings by three celebrated Menston artists: Francis Wall, Florence Mary Anderson and John Cooper.

The Ilkley Players presented several stage productions and the Society's Dramatic Art Section produced Esther McCracken's *Quiet Weekend* in March 1947. Included in the cast were some eventual 'Thespians'.

The last event of which I have any, record was in 1948 – a concert by 'Young Performers of the District' amongst whom were the pianists Patricia Hewitt, Geofrey Parker, Gillian Eastburn and Irene Fickling and a talented brother and sister John and Susan Tunnell from Guiseley. The choral section under Edward Atkinson (conductor) and Stanley Wright (secretary) met every Thursday during winter and gave several memorable concerts.

KING'S HALL, ILKLEY.

The Menston Amateur Dramatic Society

PRESIDENT - - DR. J. W. HYSLOP, J.P.

Committee:

Messrs. J. H. S. BOWES, S. H. CARTER, A. C. DOWSON, FRED G. DUNCAN, C. H. GUY, W. H. HUTCHINSON, W. H. ILLINGWORTH, ERNEST TURNER, A. C. VOIGT.

Hon. Secretary: Mr. C. M. TANKARD, Menston, Tel. 8. *Hon. Treasurer:* Mr. A. E. HASSÉ, Menston, Tel. 12.

Previous Performances—

"Boco." **"Pirates of Penzance."** **"Mikado."** **"Pantomine Rehearsal."** **"Iolanthe."** **"Patience"** **"Pirates of Penzance."** **"Dorothy."** **"Merrie England."** **"Iolanthe."** **"Gondoliers."**

The Committee have pleasure in announcing that they have arranged, with the consent of Messrs. Chappell & Co. Ltd., to produce the celebrated Comic Opera—

"Merrie England"

Composed by Edward German. Written by Basil Hood.

For Five Nights, viz., May 9th, 10th, 11th, 12th & 13th, 1922.

TO COMMENCE AT 7-30. SATURDAY, 7-15.

WITH A SPECIAL MATINÉE ON SATURDAY, MAY 13th, AT 2-30 P.M.

DRAMATIS PERSONÆ.

The Earl of Essex	Mr. W. H. ILLINGWORTH
Sir Walter Raleigh	Mr. VINCENT WARD
Walter Wilkins (a player in Shakespeare's company)	Mr. A. J. SIMPSON
Silas Simpkins (another player)	Mr. BRIAN GILL
Long Tom } Royal Foresters	Mr. R. H. WHITE
Big Ben } Royal Foresters	Mr. A. WEIGHTMAN
The Queen's Fool	Mr. J. H. S. BOWES
A Butcher	Mr. C. G. TANKARD
A Baker	Mr. STANLEY RYLEY
A Tinker	Mr. H. BREARLEY
A Tailor	Mr. HERMAN WEIGHTMAN
A Lord	Mr. NORMAN MOORE
A Soldier	Mr. CYRIL DOWSON
First Royal Page	Miss MARJORIE WHITE
Second Royal Page	Miss GWENDOLINE WHITE
Queen Elizabeth	Mrs. HAROLD C. SMEDLEY
Miss Bessie Throckmorton	Mrs. FLOCKTON FOSTER
"Jill-all-Alone"	Miss A. WHEATLEY JACKSON
The May Queen	Miss EDITH C. WOODHEAD
Marjorie	Miss BESSIE M TANKARD
Kate ...	Miss RENÉ DOWSON
Lady-in-Waiting	Miss PHYLLIS GILL
Folly Girl	Mrs. F. W. SMITH

CHORUS OF LORDS, LADIES, TOWNSFOLK, SOLDIERS, &c.

Mrs. R. Cowgill Misses E. Broadley, K. E. Clough, P. Cowling, E. Dowson, A. Dugdale, D. English, A. Exley, W. Foulds, K. Harrison, E. Kempton, L. Kershaw, K. M. Lund, W. Myers, C. Naylor, L. Naylor, S. Naylor, A. Priestman, E. Schofield, C. M. Smith, E. Smith, H. Smith, J. Smith, M. Sutcliffe, C. Terry, E. Town, A. Wells, E. Wells.

Messrs. A. Biss, C. Bullough, L. Bullough, R. Cowgill, H. J. Graves, G. S. Heaps, W. S. Heaps, L. W. Hopkins, J. L. Hornby, J. H. Imrie, H. Kempton, S. F. Lumb, H. Schofield, C. Scott, S. Scott, F. W. Smith, L. H. Verity, A. Willoughby.

Under the Stage Management of Mr. CLIFFORD PHEASEY (late Adelphi Theatre, London), and Mr. E. P. STEAD, Musical Director.

Prices of Admission—Boxes £2 2s. (including Tax);
Front Seats (Reserved), 4/- (plus Tax, 9d.); Second Seats (Reserved), 3/- (plus Tax, 6d.);
Third Seats (not Reserved), 2/- (plus Tax, 4d.); Back Seats (not Reserved) 1/- (plus Tax, 3d.).

Hon. Sec and Members will be pleased to receive orders and book seats.

Plans of Reserved Seats may be seen, and seats booked at the King's Hall, Ilkley, Tel. 155 Ilkley, on and after April 24th.

G. F. SEWELL, PRINTER, BRADFORD.

Merry England – Produced by the Menston Amateur Dramatic Society at the Kings Hall Ilkley 1922.

A Foreword

"HOUSEMASTER."

First produced Appollo Theatre, London November 12th, 1936, and ran for 663 performances. American Productions :—Opera House, Philadelphia, November 15th, 1937, Morosco Theatre, New York, January 25th, 1938, last production Theatre Royal (Church Hall) Menston, December 8th, 1938, and we hope to give three performances.

Authors note to Amateur Societies "HOUSEMASTER" is not a farcical Comedy its underlying theme is quite serious the humour of most of the characters is of the unconscious variety and should not be forced upon the audience."

Many of our friends have seen either the play or the film, and read the book but we hope that all who come to our Production will experience much pleasure and enjoyment by the efforts of our local cast.

Yours sincerely,

THE COMMITTEE.

SCHOOL GARMENTS SUPPLIED BY

Chas. H. Fox, Ltd., London.

MUSIC SUPPLIED BY

The Radio Installation Co.

Y.M.C.A. Buildings, Forster Square,

BRADFORD.

SCENERY SUPPLIED BY

Scenic Display Services,

BRADFORD.

Telephone kindly lent by the G.P.O.

CHURCH HALL, MENSTON

THURSDAY, FRIDAY and SATURDAY,

DECEMBER 8th, 9th and 10th, 1938.

at 7-45 p.m.

The Menston Thespians

in

"HOUSEMASTER"

A Comedy in Three Acts

by Ian Hay.

In aid of

MENSTON JOINT HOSPITAL FUND

and

MENSTON SICK NURSING SOCIETY.

PROGRAMME - *PRICE* 2d.

Hart & Clough, Ltd., Printers, Bradford.

Characters

in the order of their appearance

Charles Donkin	W. Foster Shepherd
Bimbo Farringdon	Colin Outtersides
Victor Beamish	C. Germain Tankard
Frank Hastings	Fred Atkinson
Ellen	Ivy Reynolds
Barbara Fane	Muriel Shepherd
"Button" Farringdon	Onaway Temperton
Matron	Janet Ellicott
Rosemary Farringdon	Marie Louise Pearson Craven
Chris Farringdon	Patricia Walter
Philip de Pourville	Michael H. Blackwell
"Flossie" Nightingale	W. Gordon Holmes
Rev. Edmund Ovington	Kenneth Younger
Sir Berkeley Nightingale	John Hannam
Travers	Wilfred Hannam
"Pop"	H. Raymond Colley
"Old Crump"	Savil Tattersall

ACT ONE.

Scene 1.–Mr. Donkin's Study in the Red House, Marbledown School.

Scene 2. –After Dinner the same Evening.

ACT TWO.

Scene 1.—Midnight—Mr. Donkin's Study.

„ 2.—Next Evening.

ACT THREE.

The Last Evening of the Summer Term.

There will be an interval of FIVE MINUTES between Act one and Act two and an interval of TEN MINUTES between Act two and Act Three.

TEA will be SERVED during the Second Interval at a charge of 3d. per cup.

Hon. Prompter: Mrs. Sylvia Roberts.

Hon. Stage Manager: Mrs. W. F. Shepherd.

The Play Produced by: W. Foster Shepherd.

President: Dr. J. W. Hyslop, J.P.

Vice-Presidents:

Mrs. Dowson. Mr. F. Wigglesworth. Mr. H. B. Kelly.

Committee: Miss E. Fletcher. Miss K. Pickles. Mr. F. Atkinson. Mrs. Shepherd. Miss M. Waddilove. Mr. A. M. Greig. Mr. A. Pickles. Mr. W. F. Shepherd.

Hon Secretary: Mr. W. Gordon Holmes, Wharfe View, West Busk Lane, Otley.

Patrons:

Mr. F. Atkinson
Mr. E. H. Barker
Mr. K. G. Barker
Mr. C. B. Barraclough
Mr. W. Barraclough
Mr. J. W. Bell
Mr. L. Booth
Mr. C. Breare
Mr. C. J. Burras
Mr. C. Butterfield
Mr. T. H. Colley
Mr. R. D. Oundall
Mr. J. A. Dobson
Mrs. E. A. Dowson
Mr. J. E Dalton
Dr. S. Edgerley
Mr. J. H. Ellicott
Mrs. J. H. Ellicott
Mr. Briggs Emsley
Mr. N. H. Farrar
Miss E. Fletcher
Mr. H. Fowler
Mr. J. H. Greaves
Mr. A. M. Greig
Mr. R. Grice
Mr. S. Harland
Mr. I. F. Harvey
Mr. S. A. Hird
Mr. W. G. Holmes
Mr. Thomas Howarth
Dr. J. W. Hyslop, J.P.
Mr. A. E. Jones
Mr. H. B. Kelly
Mr. T. K. Kelly
Mr. E. C. Kinghorn
Mr. G. R. Lawson
Mr. W. B. Lee
Mr. T. H. Moorhouse
Mr. A. Outtersides
Mr. Sydney Packett
Mr. J. P. Pearson-Craven
Mr. W. B. Pickles
Mr. F. Popplewell
Mr. G. F. Porritt
Dr. T. G. Rankine
Mr. J. Riddle
Mr. S. E. Ryley
Mr. T. H. Shaw
Mr. W. F. Shepherd
Mr. T. B. Smith
Mr. N. Snowden
Mr. G. W. Stocks
Mr. H. B. Strang
Mr. H. B. Sutcliffe
Mr. C Germain Tankard
Mr. C. M. Tankard
Mr. Savil Tattersall
Dr. D. Tillotson
Mr. J. H. Toothill
Mrs. A. Waddilove
Miss M. Waddilove
Mr. F. Wall
Mr. G. C. Walter
Mr. G. Williamson
Mr. J. M. Wintle
Mr. L. A. Wood
Mr. H. S. Woods
Mr. F. Wigglesworth
Mr. A. Young

Housemaster – Produced by the Menston Thespians 1938.

MENSTON DRAMATIC ART CLASS

present

'TO KILL A CAT'

A PLAY IN THREE ACTS
by
ROLAND PERTWEE
and
HAROLD DEARDEN

NOVEMBER 18th, 19th & 20th
1948
CHURCH HALL, MENSTON

In aid of MENSTON PARISH CHURCH
VICTORY THANKSGIVING FUND

STAGE MANAGER - Mavis Morton.

STAGE TECHNICIANS - Arthur Outtersides,
Norman Hancock,
Wilfred Hannam.

SCENERY by Dodsworth & Spencer, Bradford.

FURNITURE by Busbys, Ltd., Bradford.

LIGHTING by Stanley Edson, Otley.

'To Kill a Cat'

The Cast.

(In order of appearance).

Ruth Henley (Mrs. Proust's Secretary) .... EDNA BRIGG
Dr. Raikes (Her Private Doctor) .... BERT COOPER
Fenwick (Her Maid) .... MARGARET WILKINSON
Stella Martin (Her Stepson's Fiancee) .... JOYCE WRIGHT
Esmond Proust (Her Stepson) .... MICHAEL RYLEY
Lillian Proust .... EILEEN MITCHELL
Brand (Her Housemaid) .... JOAN AKAM
Jessop Crawley (Her Brother-in-law by an earlier marriage) .... LEONARD GREAVES
Mark Proust (Her Husband) .... FRED MASON
Whitton (Her Gardener) .... JACK PITTS

THE PLAY PRODUCED BY FRED MASON.

Synopsis of Scenes.

The action of the Play throughout takes place in the Lounge Hall of Mrs. Proust's Country House near London.

ACT I. An autumn afternoon.

ACT II. Night - 4 days later.

ACT III. An hour later.

There will be intervals of 10 minutes between Acts.

Patrons.

Mr. M. Akam
,, E. T. Bailey
,, K. G. Barker
,, E. Barrett
,, H. Bell
,, L. Bell
,, H. V. Brown
,, E. A. Busby
Mrs B. H. Butler
Mr. F. Button
,, W. Cooper
,, J. R. Cordin
,, F. Crone
Miss M. Dalby
Mr. J. A. Dobson
,, G. R. Dracup
Dr. S. Edgerley
Mr. J. R. Ellicott
,, H. Fowler
Dr. J. S. Foster
Mr. G. Galling
,, A. Gill
,, L. A. Gill
,, R. Gossop
Mrs. J. H. Greaves
Mr. J. Hearn
,, S. A. Hird
Mrs. Jagger
Mr. R. M. Jeffray
,, H. B. Kelly
Mr. O. W. Kemp
,, E. C. Kinghorn
,, L. S. Lethbridge
Mrs. Longbottom
Mr. G. V. Mackrell
,, D. H. Marchmont
,, F. Mason
,, A. S. Maston
,, J. W. G. Mitchell
,, T. H. Moorhouse
,, A. Outtersides
,, A. D. Paling
,, F. Pearson
Mrs. Pearson-Craven
Mr. A. E. Powell
,, A. E. Reddyhough
Miss Reid-Brown
Dr. R. T. Rushton
Mr. S. E. Ryley
,, W. F. Shepherd
,, G. W. Stocks
,, L. B. Sutcliffe
Miss A. Swallow
Mr. A. S. Tillotson
,, G. C. Todd
Mrs. Waddilove
Mr. G. C. Walter
Miss Winnett
,, C. A. Woods
Mr. A. Young

To Kill A Cat – Produced by the Menston Arts Class in the Church Hall 1948.

SCENERY by Dodsworth & Spencer, Bradford.

STAGE SETTINGS under the direction of Ralph Taylor.

STAGE MANAGERS:
Arthur Outtersides and Norman Hancock.

LIGHTING & MUSICAL EFFECTS by Stanley Edson.

LADIES' HAIRDRESSING by "Lillie," 1, Harrogate Rd., Rawdon.

Our best thanks go out to the cast and to these good people behind the scenes, and last, but not least, to all those who have surrendered furniture, crockery, cutlery, etc., etc., to the—
"DEAR OCTOPUS."

MENSTON DRAMATIC ART CLASS

Present

'DEAR OCTOPUS'

A COMEDY IN THREE ACTS
BY
DODIE SMITH.

MAY 9th, 10th & 11th, 1946
CHURCH HALL, MENSTON

IN AID OF
MENSTON SICK NURSING ASSOCIATION
& MENSTON JOINT HOSPITAL FUND

'DEAR OCTOPUS'

The Cast.

Charles Randolph		BERT COOPER
Dora Randolph		MARGARET WOOD
Hilda Randolph	Their Children	JOYCE WRIGHT
Margery Harvey	Their Children	DOROTHY WYNN
Cynthia Randolph	Their Children	EILEEN MITCHELL
Nicholas Randolph	Their Children	FRED MASON
Hugh Randolph	Their Children	RALPH TAYLOR
Gwen (Flouncy) Harvey	Their Grand-Children	BERYL MASON
Bill Harvey	Their Grand-Children	PETER COOPER
Kathleen (Scrap) Kenton	Their Grand-Children	NOREEN TOWN
Belle Schlesinger (Sister-in-law)		ALICE SWALES
Edna Randolph (Hugh's Mother)		EDNA BRIGG
Laurel Randolph (Hugh's Wife)		JOAN AKAM
Kenneth Harvey (Margery's Husband)		GORDON MITCHELL
Grace Fenning (Dora's Companion)		CLARE RUSHTON
Gertrude (Housekeeper)		BESSIE THOMAS

THE PLAY PRODUCED BY FRED MASON.

SYNOPSIS OF SCENES.

The action of the Play takes place at the Randolph's Country House in Essex during a weekend in Autumn. Charles and Dora Randolph are celebrating their Golden Wedding Anniversary and have gathered round them their children and their children's children.

Synopsis of Scenes.

ACT I.
The Hall. Friday Evening.

ACT II.
The Nursery. Saturday.
Scene I. Morning.
Scene II. Afternoon.
Scene III. Late Evening.

ACT III.
The Dining Room. Sunday Evening.
Scene I. Before Dinner.
Scene II. After Dinner.

Patrons.

Mr. EDWARD ATKINSON
„ E. H. BARKER
„ K. G. BARKER
„ ERNEST BARRETT
„ HARRY BELL
„ LAWRENCE BELL
„ CLIFFORD BUTTERFIELD
Dr. R. W. CARTY
Mr. & Mrs. F. CLAPHAM
Mr. R. D. CUNDALL
„ JOHN A. DOBSON
Dr. S. EDGERLEY
Mr. N. H. FARRAR
„ C. E. FOSTER
„ H. FOWLER
„ G. GALLING
Dr. R. JOHN GOURLAY
Mr. T. HAIGHTON
Rev. T. C. HAMMOND
Mr. C. A. HARDY
„ HENRY HARGRAVE
„ J. A. HOFFMANN
„ W. G. HOLMES
Miss M. ALISON JAGGER
Mr. H. B. KELLY
„ E. C. KINGHORN
„ R. LATTY
Mr. L. S. LETHBRIDGE
„ G. V. MACKRELL
„ D. H. MARCHMONT
„ F. MASON
„ A. S. MASTON
„ T. H. MOORHOUSE
Mrs. E. OLDFIELD
Mr. A. OUTTERSIDES
„ A. E. POWELL
„ F. RICHMOND
„ S. E. RYLEY
„ W. FOSTER SHEPHERD
„ W. STEWART
„ W. E. STORR
„ H. B. STRANG
„ H. B. SUTCLIFFE
Mrs. I. E. SWALES
Miss ADELAIDE SWALLOW
Mr. L. B. SWIFT
„ C. M. TANKARD
„ A. S. TILLOTSON
„ R. TODD
„ J. H. TOOTHILL
Mrs. A. WADDILOVE
Mr. FRANCIS WALL
„ H. S. WOODS
„ ANDREW YOUNG

Dear Octopus – Produced by the Menston Dramatic Arts Class in the Church Hall 1946.

SPECIAL BULLETIN NO. 32 JULY 1951

BRITISH LEGION - MENSTON BRANCH

Issued by the
Joint Secretaries
(Federation of Broken Down Builders Labourers
and Joint Butchers' Union)

Dear Member,

We are not having a Carnival this year - but wait for it - that doesn't mean you roll over for another 'kip'. Instead we are going to have a CHILDREN'S DAY and this means more work than before. We want at least 50 volunteers. These volunteers have already been chosen, so the quicker you roll up, the cushier the job you are likely to get.

There'll be something to do for anybody so don't forget the camel's hump:

The Camel's hump is an ugly hump,
Which well you may see at the Zoo,
But uglier yet is the hump we get
Through having too little to do.

Yes, dear member, we are taking care of that - "Up the Legion of the Lost" and Rally Round.

There'll be work for all men
Hayer-ho, Kul and Ficker-nay then
Can you do a job - look again men
Course you can - 'na' then then!

The foregoing versus should be la-la'd in a high falsetto to the tune of "A woman is only a woman, but a good cigar is a smoke".

	Men Required	Duty		Qualifications
(1)	4	To Police Procession Route		With waving arms and thumping big flat feet. Must have attended courses in Atomic warfare and anti-tar drill. Must be capable of putting one foot in front of the other alternately.
(2)	12	Gateman	-	Must be familiar with Treasurer's Whistle - practice in this will be given in Mr. Dalton's garden at 4 p.m. daily - parade in gaiters web and waterbottles.
(3)	1	Brass Band Skipper	-	Rope will be provided and must have an ear for music.
		(Dress - His coat is red and his breeches blue and there was a hole where his tail came through)		
(4)	2	Tape Holders	-	Must be winning "Tipsters" and able to read tickertapetenacious.
(5)	1	Starter	-	Man with pistol - iron nerves - if pistol misses fire to be prepared to use butt end.
(6)	2	Properties	-	To move obstacles from A to B and B to A according to whims of A & B., the Joint Secretaries.
(7)	2	Balloon Blower-uppers	-	Parade in Respiratos Mk IV. Must have the wind up - essential is to blow not suck.
(8)	4	Police	-	To hold back the surging masses. Nothing to breathe but air. Quick as a flash 'tis gone. Nowhere to fall but off. Nowhere to stand but on.

2.

(9)	1	Fireworks	-	Ugly - last volunteer spoilt complextion for life and has no eyebrows. After the Show he will be presented with an illuminated address.
(10)	1	I/C Punch & Judy Clowns, Bell Ringers and Magic Men.	-	Must be versatile and be prepared to substitute in case of sickness. No money in this but likely to lead to promotion.
(11)	1	I/C Pillow Fighting	-	Bring 10 Pillows and pole and mattresses, on a flat cart.
(12)	1	Instructor	-	To tell us what to do.
(13)	1	Unlucky	-	Probably you - pass on to 14.
(14)	4	Hunters	-	Treasure burying ~~Clue balking -.~~ Inventive -. Note from Treasurer: bring own Treasures.
(15)	2	Piano Movers	-	To move piano as required from time to four-time when party goes flat - Note: We have a piano.
(16)	2	Usherettes	-	To usher at evening concert - must be good looking and nifty - corsets will be issued.
(17)	1	Chucker-Out	-	Ill looking - black hair and bushy eyebrows will be looked on favourably by the Selection Board.
(18)	10	Collectors of Buttons and Foreign Coins.	-	For Collection Box at Firework Display - must respond to Treasurer's Whistle and hoot in reply.
(19)	1	Scavenger	-	To clean up Field and generally help No. 13.
(20)	21	Field Exercises	-	In field on 13th July - rig of the day running shorts (bring mosquito nets).
(21)	1	Reinforcement	-	To reinforce as necessary - to bring a cement mixer if possible.

Programme of Duties will be shown in the Post Office. See that your name is on it as it will surely be if you fill in the appended slip.

~~To: Lt. Col. H. Aurton, M.B.E.,~~
The Post Office.

Lt. Col Harry Ayrton, MBE
The Post Office

My best time is from................to................

Name......................

Address ....

....

Job preferred.........................

Special Bulletin from The British legion regarding the cancellation of Menston's Carnival in July 1951.

Interest in Art was fostered in a weekly sketching party leading to the formation of an Art Class in winter under the WRCC Education Committee. Miss Florence Anderson was the tutor.

It's fair to say, I think that the Choral Section and the Art Class were the forerunners of today's thriving groups of Singers and the Menston Arts Club.

Menston Arts Club

Founded in 1966 by a small group of Menstonians with modest ambitions, the club has now become one of the most prestigious Art Societies.

It has a waiting list for membership and the quality of work produced is such as to attract large attendances to the exhibitions held in May and November.

As I recall, the club was the brain child of the Swanns – Leslie and Audrey – who kept the DIY shop in the village and Charles Marchinton who lived at the Old School House in Main Street. Amongst the first officials were Richard Bayer, Margaret Rhodes and Harold Hall.

Percy Monkman, a wonderful 'Bradford' character and a leading watercolour artist of the day, gave the first of his many demonstrations in November of the first session and, later there were memorable visits from Angus Rands and Gordon Barlow.

Incidentally, Angus Rands, a leading Yorkshire artist, was born at Hawthorn Villa (next to Kirklands) which, for several years, was a nursing home. His mother was Agnes, a member of the well known Menston family Biss.

The first exhibitions of members' work were held in 1967 in the Menston Arms. Ted and Rose England were 'mine hosts' and relatives of club member Harold Blake.

The catalogue illustrates the beginning of a new social activity for the village which has grown over the years. From the pub, the exhibitions advanced to a room in the old Kirklands (one was actually held outside in the open air) and then, from the mid-seventies, to the Community Centre – an ideal venue for such occasions.

Besides producing the exhibition catalogues, for a short period, John Stead, a club member, was also responsible for the production of the club's own Christmas card selected from an annual members' competition.

Looking back over the years, the club has enjoyed the company of some delightful people as members, speakers, critics and demonstrators. Ben and Kathleen Done, Hextall Rawling, Peter Clark, Eric Blakey, Mollie Gardner, Jack and May Richmond, Peter Hall, Norman Watkinson (the Postmaster) and David Sharples are amongst those I remember with affection.

Norman Gedling, Peter Shutt, Peter Frank, Simon Bull, David Walker, Ashley Jackson, Barry Haste and the Ilkley duo Eric Satchwell and Bert Roberts have been outstanding contributors to the programmes. I shall never cease to wonder at the skill of the late Jon Peaty from Malton who produced such life-like portraits.

In October 1995 the club lost Paul Buckingham, regarded as its leading artist for over twenty years. Paul, who died aged eighty-four, was a past President, a frequent demonstrator, an exponent of most medias, particularly pen and wash and above all, a brilliant draughtsman.

There is now a very high standard of members' work with former President Ann Carr, the Ridyards (John and Susan) and the Waddingtons (David and Maureen) heading a long list of artists increasing the club's reputation year by year.

The Menston Singers

For twenty years, this group, led by John and Rosemary Pettitt, made a valuable contribution to the social life of the village.

Each year their concerts entertained large audiences in the Junior School hall with a wide ranging repertoire. These performances resulted in over £3000 being donated to some twenty-five charities and worthwhile causes.

Another group of singers – the Methodist Girls Choir, trained by Eleanor Cree and Sue Brown, delighted audiences in the village and further afield during the eighties.

The Menston Coronation Committee are indebted to the Local Education Committee for their permission to use the School yard and premises for the performance of the Pageant, and to all the others, too numerous to mention individually, who have given their time and assistance in the production.

Printerdom, Otley

Coronation of Her Majesty
Queen Elizabeth II

The Menston Coronation Committee presents a Pageant

"The Menston Story"

Written by J. L. Ellicott and M. Oldfield, based on the researches of Elsie M. Fletcher.

Pageant Master : Norman Stephenson
Scene Producers : R. Barker
E. Cooper
G. Dracup
Sylvia Greenwood
Rev. S. Selby
W. Senior
S. Oldfield
Stage Manager : Ralph Shelton
Asst. Stage Manager : Brian Dracup

Music by the Menston Music Circle under the direction of Mr. E. Atkinson ; Accompanist, Mrs. R. H. White ; and the Choirs of the Menston Parish Church and the Menston Methodist Chapel

Dances by the Menston G.F.S.

Fiddle Master Edgar Senior

Narrator — EILEEN MITCHELL

"The Menston Story"

Prologue

Scene 1. Tableau—An early encampment.

Scene 2. Tableau—A.D. 53—100 years after Scene 1. Cartimandua, Queen of the Brigantians.

The incident portrayed could have taken place anywhere within the domains of Queen Cartimandua, which stretched from Almondbury to Aldeburgh : History does not say where. The authors crave indulgence for their "Poetic licence" in placing the scene in this district.

Scene 3—Roman Period—A.D. 253—At the Well.
The scene is set beside the well at the bottom of Church Lane.

Scene 4. (a) Establishment of the first Chapel of Ease at Royds, about 615 A.D.
(b) Re-establishment of the Chapel of Ease, about 937 A.D.
(c) Census for compilation of Domesday Book, A.D. 1087.

Scene 5. High Hall (Fairfax Hall)—Christmas Eve—the Middle Ages.

Scene 6. May Day in the year of the Coronation of Queen Elizabeth I, 1599.
Stocks Hill and Low Hall (Menston Hall).

Scene 7. (a) High Hall, 1634—Home of Charles and Mary Fairfax.
(b) Low Hall, before the Battle of Marston Moor, 1644. Home of Richard Rhodes.

Scene 8. The Malt Shovel, about 1770.

Scene 9. On the Chevin, looking down on Menston. John Wesley.

Scene 10. Menston Villagers return from Otley Stattis (Hiring Fair)—Lane Ends, 1837.

Scene 11. Epilogue and Finale.

GOD SAVE THE QUEEN

Musical Items performed during the Pageant are as follow :-

Misere Domine
Te Deum
Minstrels Song and Carols
Now is the Month of Maying
The Rosy Dawn
Nymphs and Shepherds
All creatures now
Shepherd's Dance
Maypole Dance
Greensleeves
My love is like the Red Red Rose
Down among the dead men
Here's a Health unto His Majesty
Love is made to make us glad
England
Pomp and Circumstance
Non Nobis Domine

The Carols are early 15th century airs, attributed to John Dunstable, and obtained, by kind permission, from the Brotherton Library, University of Leeds

Above is a programme from a Coronation Pageant in 1952.

The group disbanded when the majority of the girls left home to advance their education at College or University.

A new group of singers – Ladies Please, musical director, Arnold Boddy, choir secretary Elizabeth Sharp, has been successfully established and, the Methodists again, promoted by Eleanor Cree, have formed a delightful group of singing girls and one or two boys.

Scouts and Guides

In Mrs. Heckingbottom's History of the Parish Church, the late Michael Turton contributed a brief account of the Menston St. John's Scouts between 1935 and 1971.

My earliest record of scouts in Menston shows there was a troop as early as 1909 when the Scoutmaster was Charles H. Guy, who lived in St. John's Park (Guy was a name given to a troop some years later).

I believe the 1909 troop may have disbanded at the outbreak of the First World War and was not formed again until 1935 – as recorded by Mr. Turton.

Then, I remember, the Ayrton brothers Harry and Stanley were Scout leaders and Gwen White with Mary Hargrave formed the new pack of Cubs.

Camping was always a means of maintaining interest (and probably still is) and the Scout band in the early days was also a popular feature of the group. The buglers practiced on the 'banking' – off Derry Hill and, I remember, Dick Hargrave (a future Japanese Prisoner of War) played the big drum.

Looking back, I recall the success Menston Scouts have enjoyed, particularly as several times winners of the popular Chevin Torch Race which stretched from the Jubilee Clock in Manor Square, Otley to Surprise View on the Chevin, achieved in around 6 minutes!

Scouts also had success in football and other competitions – some with Guides involvement.

Michael Turton continued interest in scout music and for many years took boys and girls to classes on Saturday mornings.

The movement prospered after the Second World War. Rev. T. C. Hammond formed a Group Committee, presided over by County Councillor I. F. Harvey. Mr Harvey inaugurated the Building Fund for the existing Headquarters in 1945. The building, in Menston Hall grounds costing around £1000, was opened in 1965.

Numbers grew in the early 70's to such an extent that another troop – Apollo was formed by Ian Drylie and Ken Chadwick. Two troops flourished during the 70's and 80's but, a few years ago a decline meant Guy troop being disbanded leaving Apollo – the survivor.

Scouts and Guides – a group which won a competition at the Annual Village Fete, 1975 *(Photograph by Jack Kell).*

Left to right – ***Back row***: Robert Kell, Nicholas Benson, Ian Brown, Chris Hunt. ***Front row***: Jonathan Cree, Judith Storr, Heidi Svensgaard, Rachel Gill, David Pratt.

A football team of scouts – Guy (1909) Troop, 1975.

Left to right – *Standing:* Nigel Melville, Andrew Husband, Anthony Hunt, Robert Kell, Nicholas Benson, Martin Thorpe (leader).
Front row: Richard Nerurkar, Jonathan Cree, Glyn Melville, Jeremy Smith, Kevin Hunt, Ian Brown.

Nigel Melville was a future England rugby union captain. Richard Nerurkar achieved international fame as a marathon runner.

In May 1975 four scouts from Menston (Guy) troop received their chief scouts award. *(Photograph by Wharfedale Observer).*

Left to right: Andrew Husband, Anthony Hunt, Scout Leader Martin Thorpe, Nick Benson and Robert Kell.

Past Guy troop leaders include Alf Howarth who was followed by the enthusiastic Thorpe brothers – Martin and Colin who were assisted by Geof Hodges. Peter Clegg was leader in 1978.

I understand the Guides and Brownies were first established in Menston in 1943 and prominent leaders have been Mrs Agnes Schofield, Mrs Nellie Dearden, Mrs. Barbara Chadwick and Mrs Pam Robertson.

Closely involved with the organisation of both Scouts and Guides were Marie Storr and the late Margaret Elsworth.

In 2007, after 15 years the Scout Leader Peter Finlay MBE was obliged to stand down and, after nearly 100 years, Menston Scouts ceased to exist.

Vigorous efforts were made and relief came in September 2009 when Charlie Baines and Ashley France, assisted by Gary Grandison, were appointed leaders.

Scouts and Guides are now under separate leadership. The District Commissioners are Roger Banister, Scouts and Sandra Newman, Guides.

The Guides and other units for junior members, are under the leadership of Sue Davidson, assisted by Debbie Hartley and Jennifer Grandison, Brownies, Beavers, Rainbows and Cromwell Cubs all have capable and dedicated leaders.

The Annual Village Summer Fete

The Annual Village Summer Fete – organised by the local Junior Athletic Club and Methodist Youth Club, ran from the early seventies to 1990, when failure to find a co-ordinator resulted in its abandonment.

In the past – for nearly a hundred years – there have been village carnivals, galas and annual sports events that have enjoyed a few years popularity and then, again, due to lack of support and organisers, have all perished.

A 'one off' Fete took place in June 1995 and was a successful occasion involving numerous village organisations. It was held in celebration of the Junior School's Centenary.

Part of the Float Procession to the village fete.

MENSTON 1902

Coronation Day celebrations at Menston commenced with a procession marshalled in front of the Board School, and containing many representatives of local bodies, in addition to school children of the village, some in fancy costumes and others on decorated machines. Many prizes were awarded.

Following the procession, tea was served to the children at the Board Schools. Later, there was a sitting down for the whole of the adult inhabitants of the village. All sat down as one family, the following ladies presiding at the tables: Mesdames J. Clayton, Exley, A. Clayton, Busfield, Hargreaves, Terry, Cheeseman, Rodgers, Peat, Taylor, Baker, Bilton, Martin, Wood, Misses Clayton, Broadwith, Hanson, Booth, Walker Halliday.

Following tea, sports were held in a field lent by Mr. Layland, and the Manningham Band played selections of dance music. Prizes for sports were distributed at the Board Schools by Mrs. McDonnell, after which the day's celebrations were rounded off by a display of fireworks in the school playground, and a bonfire on the Malt Shovel field.

The committee responsible for the arrangements for the festivities comprised Messrs. J. Crowther (chairman), W. G. Prince, J. E. Brookes, J. Clapham, J. Weightman, F. Perry, H. Woodhouse, C. J. Hartley, T. H. Moore, B. Oddy, B. Padgett, C. J. Popplewell, T. Rhodes, J. J. Wright, E. B. Voigt, E. Jones, E. H. Barraclough, S. Baker, A. Clayton, C. W. Curran, J. W. Exley, T. G. Grieg, T. H. Webb, W. Hanson, W. Bearpark, S. H. Heaps, J. E. Beaumont, H. E. Slater, E. Scott, G. White, G. Terry, W. Fletcher, J. P. Gray, J. Jackson, R. H. White, G. H. Broughton, C. Atkinson, C. M. Tankard, Dr. Hyslop, Rev. H. J. Dyer, with Mr. R. Davey as secretary.

1902 Coronation Celebrations reported by the *Wharfedale Observer.*

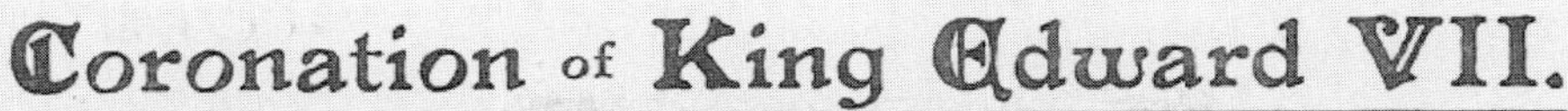

Coronation of King Edward VII.

Menstone Celebrations

WILL TAKE PLACE ON

SATURDAY,

June 28th, 1902.

A PROCESSION

In which the Guiseley Fire Brigade takes part, will be formed at the **Board Schools at 1.30** p.m., leaving at **2**, prompt.

YEADON OLD PRIZE BRASS BAND will be in attendance, and ALL RESIDENTS are requested to join the Procession.

PRIZES will be given for :—

The Best Decorated Conveyance, Two or Four Wheels.
The Best Decorated Waggon for Conveyance of Children.
The Best Decorated Cycle and Rider.
The Best Comic or Fancy Dress.

Notice is also given that every child attending the Board School will be presented with a **Coronation Half-pint Mug** by **Joseph Crowther, Esq.**, on Wednesday afternoon, June 25th.

Also a **Carter's Whip** will be given to each Waggoner conveying the Children.

A FREE TEA

WILL BE GIVEN IN THE

BOARD SCHOOL, on Saturday afternoon, June 28th, to residents over 60 years of age; to children under 15 years; and to subscribers and their families. **Children's Tea, 3.30; Adults' Tea, 4.15.**

Admission by Ticket only. For Tickets apply to the Canvassing Committee.

SPORTS & GALA

WILL BE HELD IN THE

MALT SHOVEL FIELD, at 5 o'clock, in the following order. Open to Residents in the Parish.

1.—**50 YARDS FOOT RACE, for Boys under 9 years.**
2.—**50 YARDS FOOT RACE, for Boys under 11 years.**
3.—**100 YARDS FOOT RACE, for Boys under 14 years.**
4.—**100 YARDS FOOT RACE, for Boys under 18 years.**
5.—**75 YARDS FOOT RACE, for Girls under 18 years.**
6.—**POTATO RACE, for Boys under 18 years.**
7.—**120 YARDS HANDICAP (Open).**
8.—**440 YARDS OBSTACLE RACE.**
9.—**ONE MILE BICYCLE RACE.**
10.—**100 YARDS BICYCLE RACE (Ladies & Gentlemen). Last Wins.**
11.—**100 YARDS LADIES' FLAT RACE.**
12.—**SACK RACE.**
13.—**EGG AND SPOON RACE.**
14.—**HIGH JUMP.**
15.—**PUTTING THE WEIGHT.**
16.—**TUG OF WAR.**

PRIZES MAY BE SEEN AT MR. HOLMES'S.

Entries to be made for Events Numbers 7, 8, 9, 14, 15, to Mr. J. WEIGHTMAN, Highfield View, before 7 p.m., on Friday, June 27th. Entrance Fee for these Events, **3d.** Entrance free for all other Events, open up to starting.

A Ladies' Committee will arrange Sports for Girls under 14 years of age.

The Prizes will be Presented by MRS. McDONNELL at the conclusion of the Sports.

SELECTIONS WILL BE PLAYED BY THE BAND during the Afternoon and Evening. (DANCING).

A Bonfire will be lit at 9.30 p.m., and a

Display of Fireworks, and Torchlight Procession

WILL FOLLOW.

It is requested that all Residents will do their utmost to Decorate and Illuminate their Houses. A Prize will be given for the Best.

CONTRIBUTIONS TO THE BONFIRE TO BE SENT TO THE LANDLORD OF THE MALT SHOVEL HOTEL.

All are invited to provide themselves with **TORCHES** to join the **TORCH-LIGHT PROCESSION** which meets at the **MALT SHOVEL HOTEL** at 10-30 p.m.

WM. WALKER AND SONS (OTLEY) LIMITED.

Programme for the celebration of the coronation of King Edward VII, 1902.

ILKLEY URBAN DISTRICT COUNCIL

Arrangements for the

Coronation Celebrations

AT MENSTON

MAY 12th, 1937.

9 a.m. **UNITED SERVICE** at the PARISH CHURCH.

3-30 p.m. ~~**AEROBATIC DISPLAY**~~ by Mr. G. V. Williamson of Menston. Best view to be obtained from the Menston Council School Playground.

4 p.m. **TEA** at the Council School followed by a **Punch and Judy Show, Ventriloquial Act and Pierrot Entertainment,** for all children in the Menston township under 16 years of age.

4 p.m. **TEA** at the Methodist School, followed by **Pierrot Entertainment** for Old Folks over 65 years of age.

7-20 p.m. **THE BROADCAST of the KING'S SPEECH** will be relayed by Loud Speakers at the Church Hall and the Council Schools.

MUGS. Each child up to the age of 12 years will receive a Souvenir Mug which will be presented in the Council Schools at the conclusion of the King's Broadcast.

ALL THE ABOVE ARE FREE.

6-30 p.m. **WHIST DRIVE and REFRESHMENTS** at the CHURCH HALL.

9 p.m. to 2 a.m. **DANCE with REFRESHMENTS** at the COUNCIL SCHOOLS.

Special Engagement of the—

Ambassadors Full Broadcasting Band.

TICKETS 1/6 EACH *for Whist Drive and Dance (including refreshments) may be had at the Council Offices.*

Vouchers value 7/6 will be sent to the Sick, Needy and Unemployed.

ARTHUR C. VOIGT,
Chairman of Committee.

Dixons (1930) Ltd., Printers, Guiseley & Yeadon.

MENSTON 1937

At Menston, most of the arrangements had been made with the possibility of bad weather in mind, and so events were little affected by the rain.

A morning service held in the Parish Church, was conducted by the Vicar (Rev. F. A. Hodd). The Rev. J. J. Studley (Methodist) also took part.

Mr. A. C. Voigt (Chairman of the Coronation Committee) sent the following telegram to the King:

"We, your most loyal and dutiful subjects resident in Menston-in-Wharfedale, respectfully tender to you and to your gracious Queen, our homage on your Coronation Day. May we long enjoy the blessing of your reign."

About 360 children were entertained to tea in the Council School. The tables had been brightly decorated, and tea was served in Coronation mugs, presented as souvenirs to the children. Entertainment was provided by a pierrot troupe and a Punch and Judy. The King's speech was heard through loudspeakers.

In the Methodist School, there was a gathering of some 130 people over 60 years of age, who were served with a meat tea by the "Smiling-in Committee."

A dance in the Council School and a whist drive in the Church Hall, formed the evening programme. At the dance, a singing contest attracted several entries, and the winners were Miss A. Bell and Mr. H. Jefferson. The M.C's for dancing were Dr. Rankine and Mr. E. C. Kinghorn.

Patients at Menston Mental Hospital celebrated the Coronation with a fancy-dress ball. Special decorative effects in national colours, including lighting, had been arranged by Mr. Massey (clerk of works). The M.C's for dancing were Mr. Arthur Weightman (chief attendant) and Mr. N. Hancock (deputy chief). Dr. Walker (medical superintendent) and Mrs. Walker, were present.

Coronation of King George VII and Queen Elizabeth May 1937.

The Millennium

A brief mention of Menston Millennium celebrations.

A steering committee meeting, chaired by Helen Collier, took place in July 1988.

From this meeting emerged a successful series of events and publications giving full recognition to this national milestone.

A book of Menston Walks, sponsored by Smith Settle was edited by Bill Edwards Smith and Helen Collier, maps by Jack Kell, photographs by Gordon North, Menston flora by Dr. Julian Roberts and drawings by Menston Arts Club.

A group of an older Menston people – Eric Caton, Jack Kell, Pat Reid and Ros Steel received an Age Concern Millennium Award worth £4750 – the first of such awards in the Bradford District. Pat Reid and Ros Steel produced a CD-Rom for use in schools IT Department. This project was regarded as a good partnership between the school and the older generation of the Menston Community.

Another worthwhile undertaking was the booklet *Memories, Hopes and Dreams*. This featured a number of old residents sharing their interesting memories of the village and was intended to bring old Menston to life.

The Millennium children were also asked to divulge their dreams for the future. More than 350 Menston Primary School children contributed to the book.

Menston Feast

Traditionally, for perhaps over a hundred years, Menston Feast was held in July 'the first weekend after the 16th' and old villagers averred that 'When its Menston Feast then winters at top of Chevin'.

When Main Street was little more than a country lane the Feast was held at Lane Ends in front of the Malt Shovel Hotel.

There were stalls lit with paraffin flares and a row of swings and coconut shies. Alongside the pub, in the passage or ginnel, was a shooting gallery.

As the number of amusements increased and required more space, the field behind the Hotel was taken and hundreds of visitors from the village and localities were attracted to the Feast with activities continuing into the early hours of the following morning.

Before the days of the steam traction engines and motor transport, the Feast equipment came to the village via the steep Hollings Hill pulled by horses with donkeys used as tracers.

The names of the organisers that I remember were Marshalls and Thompsons. Earlier families connected with the Feast were Baker and Murphy.

Chris Thompson came for many years, he was a showman and born in a caravan. His wife was a descendant of the famous circus family Sangster.

In the late twenties the feast moved to the Fox & Hounds to the field now mainly occupied by Brooklands.

The fairground stretched virtually from the station to the pub. Up to the footpath fence were the resplendent caravans and magnificent steam engines creating light and power. They had a distinctive oily smell but their shining polished brass and whirling fly-wheels were fascinating.

As well as roundabouts, swings, brandysnap and hoop-la stalls there were numerous side-shows containing oddities that one paid a few pence to see.

Everybody, young and old alike, seemed to visit the Feast at least once – it was a social occasion not to be missed.

I remember the weekend usually coincided with the Headingley Test Match and Bill Bowes, England's fast bowler, who lived on Bleach Mill Lane, often entertained one or two members of the team for the duration of the match.

After a hard day in the field, Bill and his guests would walk down to the Feast and, no doubt, call later in the Fox. I particularly remember Bill and Wally Keeton, England's opening batsman, shying at coconuts, 'Tek' a run at it Bill, tha' might do better' was an onlooker's advice.

Contrasting to the noise and blare of the fairground there were cricket matches on the other side of the path where batsmen were determined to loft the ball on to the 'big top'.

Saturday was a League match and on Monday evening would be a game between the President's XI and the Captain's XI containing local stars and sometimes County players.

When Brooklands appeared in the early sixties the Feast moved back to the village to the field where now stands the Primary School.

Somehow, the occasion of the Feast was never the same – it disappeared altogether for a few years when St. Peters Way was developed.

Now it arrives in a corner of Menston Hall grounds – I'm not sure when, a shadow of its former self, and perhaps goes unnoticed by most villagers.

Darby and Joan Club

This club had its beginnings during the Second World War by a group calling themselves the Smiling-in Committee.

John Marjerison, Croft House, was an enthusiastic Chairman and the old folk of the village were entertained to a Christmas Tea in the old Church Hall at Lane Ends.

The club extended its activities to a weekly meeting under the presidency of Mrs Sharpe who was followed, for many years, by Mrs Ambler. Local organisations were invited to provide the refreshments and entertainment.

After having over a hundred members, numbers began to decline – mainly due to the impact of the popular Monday and Wednesday groups formed a few years ago.

Finally, and sadly, the club disbanded in July 1997.

Presentations were made to the two faithful organisers – the president Mrs Betsy Riley, who had been actively involved with the club for nearly 50 years, and the secretary Miss Elizabeth Baines. Also, involved with this presentation was Mrs Lena Ward.

A meeting of the Darby and Joan club in the church hall 1940's

Menston's Darby and Joan Meeting with helpers.

Left to right: Mrs Mumby, Mrs Witty, Mrs Jefferson, Mrs Sharpe, Mrs Hargreaves, Mrs Hudson, Mrs Brown, Mrs Brooking and Mrs Glaister.

Darby and Joan Club Mid Fifties.

Mrs Sharpe, the president, carves the Christmas turkey. Her helpers include Mrs Garforth, Mrs Maston, Mr and Mrs Outtersides, Mrs Hird, Mrs Long and Mrs Booth.

SERVICES, SHOPS, PUBLIC HOUSES AND BUSINESSES

Menston Fire Brigade

THE first Menston Fire Brigade, directed by the Council, was formed in 1912. Albert Waite was the captain and Charlie Barnard was sergeant. Other members were George Waite, Jim Myers, Ernest Broadhead and Jack Reynolds.

The Station which housed the box-cart and appliances costing £25-7s-5d was in the Old Smithy (used as such for a 100 years) opposite the Menston Arms and now converted into an attractive dwelling – Pinfold Cottage.

Two Council reports indicate that the Brigade had some early teething troubles – 'One important thing still needed is an effective method of summoning the Brigade. A fire broke out at the weekend, but, by the time the Parish Clerk had been told and messengers had gone round the homes of the firemen, the fire was out'.

'After answering what turned out to be a false alarm at the school, Menston Fire Brigade's Captain was on the scene in five minutes, the Sergeant in six minutes and the 'box-cart' in twenty-four minutes taking another four minutes to layout the hose. It was decided to buy more hose, to ask for more water hydrants and to pay the firemen 3s (15p) for each call if they arrived on time'.

In spite of its limitations, the Menston 'box-cart' seems to have been more reliable than the Otley Brigade's horse drawn fire engine.

A 'Wharfedale Report' in 1903 reads:

> The Upper Mill at Ellar Ghyll was burned to the ground. The Otley Fire Brigade who were summoned to the fire, were delayed in starting because the two horses, which pulled the fire engine, had been put to other use by the council.

The fire had been burning an hour before the brigade arrived and found the whole building a blaze'.

The Fire Brigade's Box-Cart is from a watercolour by the late Paul Buckingham Y. W.S., produced for Menston Parish Church calendar 1995. (It is reproduced by kind permission of Mr David Whitaker who owns the original drawing).

Street Lighting

Street lighting by gas came to Menston in 1900 and the occasion was not allowed to pass without a ceremony and Guiseley Brass Band headed a procession through the village.

Two lamplighter's were paid a total of £45 per year and were instructed by the Council not to light the lamps on moonlit nights!

In 1911 there were 102 lamps in the village. Eventually the lamps were controlled by clockwork and the lamplighter's function was to keep them clean and dismantle timing clocks for the summer months when only the odd lamp was lit at road junctions. The last gas lamp disappeared in 1973.

Harry Drake. One of the villages last lamplighter's.

Village Bobbies

Menston's Law and Order, in the twenties and thirties and, probably the early forties, rested in the hands of two residential policemen.

PC Mudd lived in Stocks Hill and, at the other end of the village, in Farnley Road, was PC Geary, followed by PC George Metcalfe who rose to be a high ranking officer.

Later in Farnley Road, came PC Bowland – well respected by all sections of the community. He is involved in a story concerning Menston Cricket Club and its one time Assistant Treasurer, Bill Cooper.

Bill used to collect from parked motorists watching the cricket from the busy A65 road. After a few minutes, 'Bobby' Bowland would move them on 'for obstructing the traffic', leaving space for more of Bill's unsuspecting victims! The process would be repeated several times to Bill's sheer delight and profit to the club.

Later, in the fifties and sixties, were PC's Charlie Bennett and Norman Hunt, and more recently, PC Gordon Ellison. They were all familiar 'arms of the law' and typical village 'Bobbies' perhaps the last of a dying breed.

Post Offices

This is number 22 Derry Hill, an early village Post Office. John Clayton was the Postmaster and at one time he occupied London House by the Main Street.

An early post office in Derry Hill.

By the year 1895 Mark Bateson was Postmaster and the Office was at the end of South View. In 1910 there was a move to a more central position to the new Co-operative buildings near the school.

Mr Bateson took an active part in local affairs and was a member of the Bowling Club and an official of the local Unionist Party.

In 1920 a presentation was made to him, in the Malt Shovel Hotel, to mark twenty-five years of postal service.

In the days of yuletide benevolence to postmen, paper boys, butcher boys etc., it was said that Mark always delivered the mail himself to areas like St. John's Park and Clarence Drive on Christmas morning!

After World War II, Lt. Col. Harry Ayrton MBE just returned from the army, became Postmaster for a few years.

The new Post Office in Main Street was built in 1959. Postmasters Garrett and Baxter were in charge for short spells before Norman Watkinson assumed the Office in 1963.

Norman and his wife expanded the business to include general items of stationery and built up the reputation it enjoys today.

Norman's geniality made him a popular Postmaster and the whole village mourned his untimely passing in 1977.

Succeeding him was his son-in-law Peter Finlay who, with his wife Janet and assistants take a lively interest in village affairs and continue to fulfill all the requirements of a friendly village Post Office.

Shopping, Shops and Shopkeepers

The motor car, supermarkets and refrigeration have changed shopping habits during the last fifty years.

Before the last war few people had a fridge, not to mention a freezer and housewives shopped most days. A visit to the corner shop where you were actually SERVED was a social outing.

In addition to Menston's grocers, confectioners and greengrocers, there were at one time, three fish shops and four cobblers. Several shopkeepers like Colleys, Kendalls, the Co-op and the village butchers provided a delivery service.

Sadly, more than a dozen village shops have closed in the last ten or twenty years, mainly in the wake of the supermarkets in neighbouring Otley, Guiseley and Ilkley. They have been replaced by opticians, beauticians, accountants, insurance brokers, a nursery and, in some instances, converted to private dwellings.

For some years there were three Banking services in the village, albeit only on one day a week – the Midland at Lane Ends and Barclays (and their forerunners) at Cleasby Road. Also, I recall in my young days, the Yorkshire Penny Bank operated on Friday evenings in the Junior School. It was here I was introduced to saving my pennies by the part time actuaries (as they called themselves), Mr Harry Beaumont and Mr A S Maston.

Halifax Building Society had an agency in Cleasby Road. It is now closed, and, like the Banks – possibly for security reasons, its numerous customers have to travel outside the village to transact their business.

Following are some of the trade's people and their shops, some no longer with us, who added so much character and quality to village life.

Jack and Kate Reynolds

Jack was a well loved Menston tradesman for over half a century. He was born in 1884 and attended the village Church School paying 2d a week for lessons. Leaving school, he was apprenticed to bleaching at Joseph Gill's Rombalds Moor Bleach Works at Woodhead.

In 1910 he converted the front room of his house (previously the first Co-op premises) into a sweet shop.

When employed as a boiler man at Listers Mill in Bradford he had an accident in 1918, which resulted in the loss of his right arm. Undaunted, Jack began his green-grocery business and, until he retired in 1967, travelled round the village invariably whistling 'I'll walk beside you' with his horse and cart. 'Anything today please?' as he knocked on a door.

A story is told regarding a horse that served him well for many years. Pulling a heavy load up Cleasby Road, it collapsed and died. Surveying the poor beast as it breathed its last, Jack took off his hat, scratched his head and said 'I can't understand it, it's never done that afore!'

Jack, his horse and green grocers cart which travelled round the village.

Kate ran the sweet shop which was later built on to the front of the original property. She became a familiar and well loved figure with generations of school children who called to spend their pennies on sweets on their way to school.

Mr and Mrs Reynolds had a few years retirement before Kate died in 1971 aged eighty-three. Jack then lived another eleven years before he passed on aged ninety-eight. On their retirement in 1967, the business was run for a few years by Lily Hudson, their daughter, before the property was converted to a single dwelling house.

There were two other daughters – Marjorie who, with husband Bert Kendall ran the green grocery business in Main Street between Farnley and Bingley Roads.

Ivy and husband Ossie Weyman kept the village store at Burley Woodhead for many years.

Reynold's fruit and sweet shop and stable for Jack's horse.

Menston Fruit Store

Originally built as a house and shop by Ronnie Jones in the thirties. His father, Walter, had a market garden behind the shop, extending through to Cleasby Road.

The Kendals, Bert and Marjorie (nee Reynolds), followed in the mid forties until 1971, when Alan and Edna Jennings acquired the business. They extended the shop and were popular green-grocers for ten years.

Alan and Gwenda Jenness succeeded them but after a time, like some other village traders, they suffered from the impact of supermarkets in nearby towns. In 1991 they gave up the business and converted the premises into a private house.

Menston Fruit Store in Main Street (opposite the park).

Henry Hargrave

One of Menston's best known personalities in the first half of the last century earned for himself the title of 'Mr Menston'.

He came to the village from Skipton in 1879 with his parents and a family of ten children. Henry at this time was a few months old. His father was a shoemaker – a trade which he eventually passed on to Henry. The house the family moved into what was known as 'Church House' in Derry Hill where for a time the Anglicans worshipped before St. John's was built.

The cobbler's business was carried on in several premises before moving to London House in Main Street. The shoe business eventually declined and until Henry retired in 1963, Hargraves was a typical English 'corner shop'.

Henry attended the Church School at Lane Ends and became an all-round sportsman. He was successful at both football and cricket with the village clubs and won several trophies at both sports.

He was a lifelong member of St. John's Parish Church, serving in the Choir and as a Church Warden. During the War he was a Special Constable and a founder member of the Darby and Joan Club.

Henry Hargrave – 'Mr Menston'.

For many years, Henry was a local Councillor serving on the old Menston Parish Council then the Wharfedale RDC and his public duties culminated in his election to the chairmanship of the Ilkley Urban District Council in 1942-43.

Henry's son, Dick, was a brave survivor of brutal captivity by the Japanese in World War II. He was in a camp where out of 2700 prisoners, only 400 came out alive.

Henry Hargrave's shop, London House, Main Street, Menston.
Dick's Garth Road on the right.

Arthur and Ada Outtersides

A well respected Menston couple who made valuable contributions to the business, public and social life of the village for over half a century. They ran Cadema Bakery and confectioner's shop in Bradford road (now an antique shop) established by Ada's father Henry Brown in 1901.

Ada claimed to be Wharfedale's first woman driver, delivering bread in a 2.3 horsepower Ford T type van. She was taught to drive by Willy Settle the ambulance driver at the Children's Isolation Hospital. She taught several other women to drive who became ambulance drivers in the Great War including Dorothy Bennett who later ran a taxi business (I remember Dorothy transporting the cricket club's second XI members to away matches as far as Sowerby Bridge and Knaresborough).

Arthur, outside business, was a member of the old Menston Parish Council and later, the Ilkley Urban District Council. He was Special Constable, a founder member of the Ilkley and District Motor Club and a leading member of the British Legion Players who preceeded the present Thespians.

Both Ada and Arthur served on the Darby and Joan Committee and were awarded the British Legion Gold Medal for outstanding achievement in that institution.

Ada ended her life as an invalid – a very cheerful invalid spending most of her time in bed, near a window in their home on Leathley Road.

She was always 'Mrs Outtersides' to me and for several years I waved to her on my way to work. If ever I was distracted, or in a hurry, and didn't wave, I heard about it!

379

'PHONE 73. BRADFORD ROAD, (CADEMA BAKERY),

MENSTON, 6 June 1927

M Wesl. Sunday School

Bought of A. OUTTERSIDES,

High-Class GROCER, BAKER and CONFECTIONER.

No.	Goods	Entry	£	s.	d.
1	Home-made Potted Meat.	6 Doz Tarts		6	0
2	Sausage and Pork Pies.	6 " Buns Cream		6	0
3	Cooked Ham and Tongue.	6 " Coc Buns		6	0
4	Best Grades of Tinned Fruit.	1 " Tea Cakes		1	0
5	Fish and Meat Pastes (Shippham's).	12 lb Butter		2	4
6	Tinned Salmon, Crab and Lobster.	½ lb Tea		1	4
7	Tobacco and Cigarettes.	4 lb ~~Butter~~ Sugar		1	5
8	Tea and Coffee (various makes).	3 Sand Loaves		2	6
9	Jams and Lemon Cheese and Marmalade.				
10	Cadbury's and Terry's Chocolate.		1	6	7
11	Best Makes of Biscuits.				
12	Finest Currants and Sultanas.	Paid			
13	Brown Breads, Bermaline, Cadema Malt, etc.	26 June 1927			
14	Dairy and Danish Butters.	[illegible]			
15	High Quality Bread and Milk Bread fresh daily.				
16	Afternoon Tea Fancies.				
17	Pastry and Cakes fresh daily.				
18	Highest Grade White Flour.				
19	Turog and Allinson's and Hovis Wheatmeal.				
20	Muffins and Crumpets.				
21	Jewsbury and Brown's Table Waters.				
22	Sole Agent for Energen Breads and Energen Dietetic Products.				

SPECIAL TERMS FOR WHIST DRIVES, PARTIES, &C.

Telegrams: 'Metodico, Cent. 'Phone, London
Cables: 'Metodico,' London.
Codes: A.B.C., 4th, 5th and 6th Edns.

...HOUSE,
...DON, E.C.4 17/6/27 192
...TON
...GEORGE.

...d Postal Orders should be made payable to ...TON, crossed Midland Bank, Ltd., and addressed ...W. Morton George, Ludgate Circus House London, E.C.4.

8 0
[illegible]
9
9" 9

Bill for goods supplied to the Sunday School in 1927.

Arthur and Ada Outtersides

Richmonds

This is the property at the junction of Main Street and Upper Cleasby Road, known for many years simply as 'Richmond's' or appropriately, Grosvenor House.

On the left is the shop run by Mrs Richmond and her two daughters Lucy and Jessie as genteel ladies' haberdashers (Mrs Richmond's brother was Mark Cowling, a well known Menston builder. He built Hawksworth's Methodist Chapel).

The butchers were Robert (Bob) and sons Mark and Frank, all sportsmen, particularly Frank who was an outstanding member of a successful Otley Rugby Union side in the thirties and a very useful batsman for Menston.

The family lived on the premises and they, and their businesses, were an asset, giving grace and character to the village.

I am indebted to Mrs Susan O'Neill, Mark's daughter, for the photograph on page 160.

Richmonds – Grosvenor House.

The Chemist's Shop

Here is Martin Brown the chemist in 1980 with two of his staff celebrating eighty years of the village pharmacy.

Grosvenor Terrace was built in the 1890s and the shop originally faced west into Cleasby Road, its width little more than the window shown on the right of the photograph. The chemist lived in the premises which now constitute the shop.

The late Tom Wood, an old Menstonian, said his mother remembered it first as a butcher's shop with dressed lambs hanging on iron hooks. These hooks can still be seen outside the unused west door.

It became a pharmacy about the turn of the century when the chemist was John Naylor (he appears in Robinson's Directory of 1904) before W B (Billy or Bertie) Lee who advertised the business in the Directory of 1909.

For nearly seventy years the pharmacy was in the hands of just two chemists first Mr Lee and then Hugh D Brown who came immediately after the Second World War, initially in partnership with Maurice Midgely.

The Brown family moved to live in a house in Cleasby Road in the early 1950s allowing the shop to be extended to its present size. The village was saddened by Hugh's sudden death at the age of sixty-three in 1981.

The business is now in the hands of Cohens who both accept prescriptions and deliver them.

The chemist's shop Martin Brown and two assistants celebrating 80 years of pharmacy in Menston..

Main Street and Cleasby Road junction about a hundred years ago showing the chemist shop on the right as it was originally.

Sam Biltcliffe, Butcher

His shop was originally in Stocks hill opposite the Methodist church – now a private house. A popular butcher, he had an assistant, George who also delivered orders.

Incidentally, he gave me, a 12 year old, my first paid employment – delivering meat on Saturday mornings for the princely sum of 6 pence and a pork pie!

A story is told of Sam's involvement in a British Legion sponsored whist drive, sometime in the thirties. It was usual, in this period, for prizes to be given by local people and he undertook to be responsible for a prize that would be worth a guinea. The recipient was not a little disappointed to receive a box of Beecham's pills which according to the advert of the day, to be 'worth a guinea a box'.

In the mid thirties, Sam moved across the road to a new shop and house where he was eventually followed by Frank Button, Douglas Thornber and until 2002, by Barry Jackson.

The property was the first in an open field to be followed by the new post office (1959) the Methodist Manse (1960) a private house, the parade of shops and flats and, finally, in the sixties, Croft Park.

Barry was the last of the village butchers – Joe Vickers in Derry Hill and those who followed Richmond's closed earlier. Barry's faithful customers were all sorry to lose him and the cause was hard to accept. It was suggested that the new 'one stop/shop' supermarkets were being preferred by many shoppers, including Menston's.

Some other shops I remember were, at Lane Ends, Mrs Appleton, a busy little woman selling sweets and confectionery, and a sequence of newsagents – Leslie Bateson (son of the Postmaster), Robinsons and Uptons where the vital 'Pink' Yorkshire Sports paper was collected on Saturday evenings. On the opposite side of the road was Lumbs the grocers.

The Co-operative Stores – with its solid wooden counters down each side, where, amongst those who served, were the Manager Mr William Roberts in a long white apron and flat cap and, with inexhaustible patience, Miss Mabel Biss. Behind, dealing with incoming supplies was

Helliwell's village store. Alan Horsman and George Foster.
Note: the cottages on the right were where the famous evangelist Smith Wigglesworth was born.

Church Lane – the shop – 'Fish and Rabbit Salesman'.

Corner of Main Street and Derry Hill – now Menston Arms car park.
This shop, in my youth and, I believe, into the early sixties, was the village fish shop. Alan Jennings rode his bike up the steps to buy his pennorth of chips!

Mrs Cowgills drapers shop in Derry Hill – 1945.

Francis Chipman. I remember Bert Hill, as strong as a horse, delivering the groceries to all parts of the village and beyond. Regular customers had a 'check number' which was recorded against each purchase for eventual 'divi' paid yearly.

The 'Bridge' shops on Bradford Road were Outtersides and their Cadema Bakery, Bells (paint and wallpaper) and Lumbs (grocers) who were followed in the thirties by Colleys.

At the end of South View were Clifford Smith, a cobbler, and another typical corner shop – 'Bearparks' who were followed by Mrs Anderton.

On the corner of Cleasby Road and Main Street, the grocers I recall were Spence followed by Matthews, before Jim Dyson and son Alan. The early shop keepers in Cleasby Road are recorded on page 155. The Whitehouse newsagents at the Fox and Hounds closed in 2001 after 50 years in business.

Laurie and Nellie Rawlings Marlborough Dairy

Two familiar Menston personalities – Laurie and Nellie Rawling. They took over the business from Laurie's father William who retired due to ill health, in 1928 and they were selling milk for forty-one years until 1969.

The business operated under the name Marlborough Dairy and was originated by a man named Scott who lived in Marlborough Cottages. He farmed the adjacent land, now Leathley Avenue and Crescent and sold his products from a shop in Cleasby Road.

The Rawlings transferred to Dicks Garth Road but retained the name Marlborough Dairy and the milk was supplied by Nellie's father Jack Lancaster of Hagwood Farm in Bleach Mill Lane.

An old Menstonian, Tom Wood who, as a boy, delivered milk told the story of a lady who always insisted on having milk for her children from one particular cow. The farmer delivered it in a special can. What the lady never knew however, was that the milk had only been transferred from a large can at the end of the road and was the same milk as was delivered to all the other customers.

Laurie and Nellie Rawling.

Long before our present age of supermarkets, other suppliers of milk round the village – usually twice a day, were Scotts of Derry Hill Farm (followed by Arthur Gott), Jack Binner (who followed the Cassons), Herbert Spencely, Oaks Farm, Alby Knowles, Chevin Grange Farm, Jos Pickering New House Farm and John Turner, Well House.

The only survivor of these 'traditional' milkmen is Richard Hill who, early and faithfully, still delivers fresh milk to village doorsteps.

'Pots or Lamp Oil'

The cry by which Maurice Garforth was recognized in the streets of Menston and much further afield in Wharfedale and Airedale. Maurice was the last of four generations who carried on a family business selling household goods, hardware and paraffin which spanned over 140 years.

The business was started by his great grandmother who lived in Shipley and travelled on foot, selling pots and pans from a basket. His grandfather

Maurice Garforth and his wagon.

Sam used a mule and cart to carry his wares, and his father, another Sam, swopped the mule for a horse.

When Maurice took over the business in the mid thirties he used a model T Ford Waggon from which he exchanged pots and basins for rags. In his 'boom' years he was selling 50,000 gallons of paraffin a year. He retired in 1973 and died aged sixty-nine in Cumberland in 1980.

Village Public Houses

In his book on *Menston and Hawksworth*, Alastair Laurence has researched the history of the village public houses and provided interesting information.

I recall the stone buildings of the old Hare and Hounds which included a glass roofed area over a cobbled yard where one could wait for a bus on the A65.

Robert Foulger was the innkeeper and had a racehorse named after him. Behind the pub was the Menston bowling green which, for several years, was tended by my grandfather.

In the late 1930s the stone buildings were demolished and replaced by the modern brick built hotel which has recently been extended.

The original Hare and Hounds from a painting.

The second Hare and Hounds – replaced 1939.

The long established and popular Malt Shovel Hotel (c1850), as its name suggests, is reputedly associated with the old malt kilns in the fields near Derry Hill where once barley grew.

The Malt Shovel.

The Menston Arms.

The youngest pub – the Menston Arms, which now displays the Arms of the Fairfax family, was for many years without a licence to sell spirits and known simply as the Beerhouse. In an earlier age, it was identified locally as 'Jerry's Oile'.

The Fox & Hounds Hotel (now the Fox) one of Menston's oldest pubs. According to old Menstonians it was originally located in the village where the steps to St. John's Church are.

Our photo from the 1960's shows a Sammy Ledgards Leeds - Ilkley bus and on the right is Netherby where lived centenarian Thomas Buck. He died in 1926, aged 103. Ronnie Biss, former Editor of the *Wharfedale Observer* tells the story that Mr. Buck married for the second time at St. John's and was 92. When he reached 100 he had a new suit made and insisted that there should be two pairs of trousers!

The Fox and Hounds in the 1960's.

The Chevin Inn on the old main highway to Otley, the first inn was there in 1646. The barn on the right was an early Methodist meeting house. Church records describe it as the 'Shivinthend' Class which met there.

The Chevin Inn.

Menston Garage

It's beginnings were uncertain but I understand it was incorporated as a Company in 1919. Two names are mentioned James Crowe, Engineer and George Frederick Underwood, Solicitor.

The flourishing business was established in 1933 when the Pitts family came to Menston. Walter was appointed Manager under the ownership of Harry Wilson.

At this time there was a single hand operated pump and, I recall the garage was illuminated by a brilliant neon sign which could be seen for miles around.

In 1955 Walter was joined by his sons Jack and Harry, later by Brian, who all became Directors of the firm.

The Company took the Vauxhall franchise in 1964 and rapid expansion began.

Jack died in 1978 before the new showroom was completed. The third generation of the Pitts family business included Roger, Keith, Stephen and Colin. Sadly, and unexpectedly, Colin died in 1990 at the early age of 38.

An early Menston Garage advertisement.

Roger was the managing director when the firm was taken over by Dixons in 2000. Brian died in 2003.

In 2007 Dixons closed several of their garages. Unfortunately, this included Menston.

The site was taken over by JCT 600 and opened in 2010.

Waites Garage Bradford Road

The business was started in 1902, by the brothers Albert and George Waite.

They began as Electrical Engineers in a little green wooden hut – in Station Road. The land had been purchased by their father Mr Isaac Waite (the first Chief Engineer at Highroyds Hospital) from Mr Phillip Padgett.

Albert and George commenced their business part time, mainly fitting lighting conductors, installing electric bell systems in large houses from storage cells and also selling and repairing bicycles.

The business of Waite Brothers prospered and as the Motor Car and Cycle industry developed, in 1913 they had the garage built on the Main Road.

Eventually, Albert went to the Asylum as chief mechanic and George's son Horace succeeded him in the business.

Waite Brothers were pioneers of the motor car business in this area theirs was the only Garage between Sharp & Griffiths at the foot of Hollings Hill and the Maypole in Otley and between S & G and Ilkley. The petrol supply came by rail in cans and casks to Menston Station. The cautious Station Master, Mr Lintern, always insisted that the wagons carrying the petrol should be shunted as far away from the station as possible.

George (affectionately known as 'chinny') and son Horace, carried on the business successfully for many years earning a great deal of respect from the motor car industry, local motorists and cyclists.

Eventual occupiers of the premises were Henry Hudson and Menston Garage. It is now a Golf Accessories Shop.

The wooden premises in Station Road where Waite Brothers started their business.

Waite's Garage in Bradford Road (Station Garage) on the left is Albert with father Isaac. The car is a Standard c1929-30.

W. JONES,
Hairdresser.
WHOLESALE and RETAIL TOBACCONIST.
CLEASBY ROAD.
Telephone No. 194.

MARGARET M. JONES,
Hairdresser.
PERMANENT WAVING and all Branches of HAIRDRESSING.
Beauty Parlour, Carlbourne Villas.
Telephone No. 194.

"LEAVE YOUR WORRIES HERE" . . .
MENSTON GARAGE LTD.
'Phone 72 Menston.
Minor Adjustments, Cylinder Regrinds, Complete Overhauls.
Breakdown Ambulance Available Day or Night.
BATTERY CHARGING and REPLATING. WIRELESS BATTERIES COLLECTED, CHARGED and DELIVERED WEEKLY.

W. B. LEE, M.P.S., PHARMACIST, CHEMIST (By Examination).
Physicians' Prescriptions Carefully and Accurately Dispensed.
RELIABLE DRUGS ONLY KEPT IN STOCK. WINES & SPIRITS OF THE BEST BRANDS.
CLEASBY ROAD, MENSTON.

G. HARDISTY,
CLEASBY ROAD, MENSTON.
High-class CONFECTIONERY.
COOKED MEATS. HOME-MADE JAM.

MISS JOAN SYKES,
HAIRDRESSER and BEAUTY CULTURIST,
Grove Villa, Main Street, Menston.
Registered Eugene Waver.
Tel. 180 Menston.

CADEMA BAKERY (MENSTON) LTD.
Secretary: A. Outtersides, Fel. Inst. B.B.
High-Class BAKERS and CONFECTIONERS,
BRADFORD ROAD, MENSTON. Telephone 73.
FRESH BAKED BREAD and CONFECTIONERY DELIVERED DAILY.
Wedding and Birthday Cakes made to order. Fancy Cakes for Afternoon Teas, etc.
We Specialise in Catering. Established over 30 years in the Village.

H. ROBINSON,
STOCKS HILL BAKERY,
MAIN STREET, MENSTON.
Tel. 276.
PRACTICAL BAKER and CONFECTIONER.

FRED HOPPER,
DERRY HILL, MENSTON.
FISH, FRUIT and POULTRY SALESMAN.
FRESH YORKSHIRE RABBITS.
CUT FLOWERS.

Local business people, printed 1940.

LAWRENCE BELL & SON,
N. F. M. P.
High-Class Painter, Decorator and Contractor,
HOUSE and CHURCH DECORATOR.
The House for Quality.
Pattern Books sent on Request.
BRADFORD ROAD, MENSTON
Tel. : Menston 71.
Also at 1, ASH GROVE.

'PHONE 186. ESTIMATES FREE.
S. AYRTON, R.P.C., M.I.P.
REGISTERED PLUMBER & CONTRACTOR.

High-class Workmanship in Modern Bathroom Fitting.
Central Heating. Roof and all Property Repairs.

Residence: GRANGE AVENUE, MENSTON.

T. H. COLLEY, GROCERIES AND PROVISIONS,
Bridge Store, Bradford Road, : : MENSTON.
High Quality only in all our Goods. Service and Satisfaction.
Deliveries in all Districts. A Trial Solicited.

TEL. 234. SEND A POSTCARD OR 'PHONE FOR OUR TRAVELLER TO CALL.

CHARLES LAND,
CLEASBY ROAD, : : MENSTON.
Agent for K Shoes. Reliable Boot Stores.

REPAIRS. WORKMANSHIP GUARANTEED. HAND-SEWN WORK A SPECIALITY.

TELEPHONE 50 MENSTON.

J. REYNOLDS,
HIGH-CLASS FISH, FRUIT and POULTRY SALESMAN,
MAIN STREET, MENSTON.

Telephone No. 63 Menston.
R. RICHMOND,
FAMILY BUTCHER,
CLEASBY ROAD, MENSTON.
Prime English-Fed Beef and Mutton selected and killed by myself.

MENSTON LAUNDRY
Main Street,
MENSTON.
HIGH-CLASS WORK A SPECIALITY.
DRY CLEANING. DYEING.
Telephone :
MENSTON 78.
PRICE LIST OF ALL SERVICES ON APPLICATION.
Proprietors :
E. WHITE & SONS, LTD.

IF YOU WANT THE
CLEANEST, HOTTEST AND CHEAPEST
COAL
IN THE DISTRICT, TRY
Tel. Guiseley 542
C. A. HARDY.
Res.: WEST END TERR., GUISELEY.
Depot: STATION YARD, MENSTON.

Local business people, printed 1940.

PLAYING FIELDS AND SPORT IN MENSTON

Playing Fields

UNTIL Mr Clifford Butterfield presented the Menston Hall grounds to Ilkley UDC in 1962, (which is now the well used, and loved, Menston Park) village children played their games in the streets or trespassed on some farmer's land.

Between the wars, at least in the twenties, with little motorized traffic, it was possible to play cricket even in Main Street. There were some interruptions – from an occasional car and, every half hour, from the village bus.

Eventually, for a half crown subscription, junior members of the Cricket Club were allowed to play on the edge of the field at the Fox and Hounds. Tackle was very basic – a bat, a ball and stumps. We had no pads, those whose shins required protection stuffed dock leaves down their stockings.

I recall one occasion when a 'test match' was being played under the high wall adjacent to the A65 road. That day we were using a new cricket ball – a present from my grandmother. It was a bright red 'corky' and cost 6d from Woolworths.

About halfway through the first innings, the ball was lofted over the wall on to the road. Just as two or three fielders had scaled the wall to retrieve it, a West Yorkshire bus – a double decker, came up the road going to Bradford.

Suddenly it slowed down and stopped long enough for the conductor to step off the platform at the back and pick up the ball from the gutter. Jumping back, he rang the bell and away went the bus with our ball, bringing summary abandonment of our cricket match.

What was, I think, my first letter of protest was addressed to the West Yorkshire Road Car Co. explaining what had happened and giving an approximate time the bus passed the ground.

A few weeks later I received a letter of apology from the manager indicating that both conductor and driver had been suspended from duty and the ball – (costing sixpence) could be collected from his office.

Football was played in several fields. One typical was Charlie Wormald's between Derry Hill and Moor Lane (there is still a footpath through from the top of Dick's Garth Road). Charlie's farm was Hill Top which could clearly be seen several fields away.

Jackets and jerseys were the goal posts, makeshift teams were chosen and the game proceeded. It was only brought to a premature end when Charlie was spotted, stealthily making his way down the fields. Not until he appeared on the edge of our pitch would the ball and 'goal posts' be gathered up to make a quick getaway, leaving Charlie waving his stick and threatening dire punishment.

I remember one such occasion when either the ball or a jacket had been left behind in our haste to leave. It was Colin Newstead who 'drew the short straw' to walk up Moor Lane to Hill Top and knock on Charlie's door.

For several years, in the twenties, the matter of a Playing Field was discussed by the Parish Council. For one reason and another mainly expense, it was repeatedly shelved.

In March 1933 there was a Public Meeting of Rate-payers in the Junior School. The Chairman, Mr A C Voigt, indicated that the Council had considered three plots of land to purchase but, in each case, they were regarded as being too costly.

The areas considered were:

1. 'Butterfield's' land – behind the Hare and Hounds Hotel (now Leathley Crescent and Glen Dene) 5.7 Acres at 2s 6d (12 ½ p) a square yard.

2. 9 Acres behind the Junior School at 11d (less than 5p) a square yard.

3. 3 ½ Acres – The Brooklands Estate at 1s - 6 ½ d (7 ½ p) a square yard. Brooklands was offered to rent but was considered to be too remote from the village.

Mr A S Maston, headmaster of the Junior School contended that the majority of the Rate-payers would not object to a penny a week on their rates for 300 children of the village to play in a field.

The Rate-payers present, however, decided by a three to one majority that it would be 'unfair to increase the rates that could be anything between ½ d and 3d'.

There was still more procrastination when Menston was absorbed in to the new Ilkley UDC in 1937. Then came the Second World War and the whole subject of Playing Fields was postponed until Mr Butterfield made his generous offer in 1962.

Sport in Menston

Cricket, football, tennis, bowls and hockey have all been, or are being, played in the village.

There is also evidence of a Menston Golf Club (the course was on Ilkley Moor) and, although rightly claimed by Burley, at the bottom of Menston Old Lane on the side of Bradford Road, was a race-course.

Snooker is still being played at the well established Men's Clubs in Main Street and Farnley Road.

In more recent years a Badminton Club has been formed, playing in the Community Centre.

Today's thriving Junior Athletic Club was founded in 1973. Wilf Sheffield, landlord of the Menston Arms, was President and other officials were George Wheelwright (schoolmaster), Arthur Robinson, John Joyce and Ernie Brown.

Football

Miss Fletcher records that Menston's first football team rejoiced in the name 'Menston's New Delight'. That was about a hundred years ago and there followed a 'Menston United' and later, the team was simply 'Menston'.

In these early days the club's headquarter were in the Menston Arms and amongst members were old village names – White, Hargrave, Hancock and Emmott.

Henry Hargrave was Captain and Secretary and in 1905, was generously presented with a gold watch in recognition of his services.

The team had varying fortunes but 1908 was a disastrous season when not a single point was gained in sixteen matches.

About 1911, when the Parish Church vicar Rev. E. R. (Dickie) Dawe, a keen sportsman, became President, the Club was named Menston St. John's – a title that persisted long after sponsorship by the church ceased.

The first ground was behind the Malt Shovel Hotel where, earlier, cricket and knur and spell had been played. The changing room was in the Church Hall although generally, most players went to, and came from, a match in their sportswear under an overcoat.

My own memories of Menston football stretch to the late twenties when St. John's played in a field opposite the existing Hillside Court in Derry Hill.

There were two teams playing league football and some of my heroes were Leslie Gill, Laurie Shaw, Harry Dyson, Harry Hollings, George and Dick Jefferson and Herbert Bearpark.

Fixtures against Addingham (known as the Tigers) and Burley Trojans were always needle matches.

The club disbanded in 1931 but, after five years, a group of village youths were responsible for its revival – playing on what was known as White's Laundry field (now occupied by Moorfield Avenue).

Arnold Kempton, Arthur Bearpark, Stanley Morse, Maurice Biss and Stanley Atkinson were members of the group. Players included Wilson Wright, Alan Jennings, Bert Hill, Dennis Cowgill and Fred Brooking.

Perhaps the club's most famous player was goalkeeper Jim Newton who played at this time. As a retired professional, Jim had recently assisted Coventry City and Brighton and Hove Albion.

Another ground was used in the late thirties – the field at the junction of Derry Hill and Bingley Road.

After the war in 1946-7, Arthur Bearpark, who was to gain an award for fifty years meritorious service to the game, inspired a new interest in the club. St. John's vicar, Rev. T. C. Hammond was elected President and he was supported by several local worthies as Vice Presidents.

League football was played first in the field now occupied by the Brooklands Estate and then on Main Street, where stood Heather Court and is now Ling Court.

It was here in 1957 that Harry McIlvenny, who had represented England at centre forward as an amateur, appeared on the team sheet.

Menston St. John's A.F.C. 1921.

Not all the members can be identified but amongst those standing are: Stanley Dyson, Rev. E. R. Dawe (vicar), Alan Rawling, Sam Exley, Arthur Hannam, Clifford Barfield, Frank Horsman and Percy Davey. ***Seated***: Harry McKinley, Maurice Baker, Syd Moon and Frank Hall. ***Front row:*** Laurie Shaw and Albert Habishaw.

The photograph was by Miss Sampson – her studio was on the site of former workshop of Menston Garage.

I believe it was that year that St. John's reached a cup final and lost to Burley Trojans at Guiseley.

Football field and Willow House Farm, Main Street, now
St. Peters Way and where stood Heather Court.

St Peter's Way with flats and Infant's school built on the
football field site (above). Willow House Farm, right centre shrouded by trees.

For two or three seasons the club had to play on the Burley Trojans ground until the final move was made to Menston Hall in 1964 on the playing field presented to the village by Mr Clifford Butterfield, two years earlier.

The club carried on until 1982 when it became difficult to maintain the policy of playing Saturday afternoon football.

Since 1982 the ground and the dressing rooms have been used almost continuously by various teams, mainly juniors.

Bowls

Bowls was played from the 1890s to around the mid nineteen thirties by a well organised club behind the Hare & Hounds Hotel.

Several domestic trophies were annually competed for and opposition came from clubs as far away as Bradford, Leeds and Harrogate.

Amongst the members were Dan Clayton, T. H. Webb, J. T. Cole and Joe Greetham. Harry Gill of Willow House Farm combined bowls with cricket and was elected a Life Member of Menston C.C. in 1945.

The present Bowling Club was established in 1954 when the Bradford Metropolitan Council laid a new crown green, for public use behind Kirklands.

Councillors Harry Bell and Arthur Outtersides with Ronnie Collins (the first President) were mainly responsible for the club's formation.

Until the clubhouse was built, members met in the spartan conditions of the old seventeenth century barn, where swallows nested in the timbered roof.

The club continues to prosper with both men and women competing in local League and Cup competitions.

Tennis

A tennis club was formed in 1888 and there were three courts behind Fourness House (now Kirklands), the home of Mr Joseph Exley, J.P.

It was disbanded in 1912 when the effects of the club were sold by auction. It was stated that the club's demise was 'largely due to the remarkable progress of golf'.

The tennis I remember was played at White's in Main Street where now stand semi-detached houses in Moorfield Avenue.

The club was founded in the early twenties by Dick White, Manager of the Laundry.

There were two shále courts and one grass. Round the perimeter was a putting green.

The clubhouse was an old yellow trackless tramcar and some players, I recall, were John Smith, Jack Heron, Cherry Dean, Dorothy and Len Turner, Jeffray Weightman, Stanley and Gwen Morse and three White sisters, Kathy, Joan and Peggy.

The Methodist Tennis Club has been in continuous existence since the nineteen twenties, when a court was used at Mr Haley's house in the Homestead. Then for a few years, the club played on a grass court in the grounds of Cadema Bakery in Bradford Road.

In 1937, a new court behind the Church, costing £164, was opened by Mr Charles Tankard and Mr Andrew Young.

Maurice and Gladys Baker and Norman Atkinson were founder members and the Pitts family has had a long connection with the club.

Doris Holmes achieved the distinction of being a playing member for over 50 years.

Hockey

The Hockey Club, as I recall, existed only for a few years – in the late twenties and early thirties.

St. John's was its base and the team consisted largely of G.F.S. members. Amongst the girls were old Menston names – White, Reynolds and McKinley.

They played on White's Laundry field and, for a couple of seasons, on the cricket field at the Fox & Hounds. Here they were not charged any rent but offered their services in tea-making for the cricketers in summer.

Horse Racing

The Burley Racecourse was on the left hand side of Bradford Road from the junction with Otley Road to a point opposite Menston Old Lane.

According to the Wharfedale Observer, a reader Mr Arthur Thorne, produced a race card dated 19th October, 1869.

The longest race was about 1 ½ miles and the races that day were the Inn Keepers Plate (15 sovereigns), Wharfedale Handicap (22 sovereigns), Stewards Cup (10 guineas), Farmers Stake (10 sovereigns) and the Consolation Stakes (5 sovereigns) for beaten horses.

Golf

Evidence of a Menston Golf Club (again, is supplied by the *Wharfedale Observer*).

'Two trophies' were found, some years ago, in the bar of Ilkley Golf Club. The first was a magnificent shield called the Menston Shield, 1895.

No clue as to its standing in the past, but it is thought that it belonged originally to the 'Old Menston Golf Club'.

Menston Cricket Club

Some of my earliest memories.

Seeing Mr Willis' sheep, on the field, keeping the grass down during winter months.

The primitive conditions of the pavilion which had been improvised from a farm house – the stables on the ground floor and living quarters above.

There were no toilets (there was a privy in the pub yard).

Committee meetings in winter were held in candlelight.

In the early fifties, when both first and seconds, led by Eric and Jack Thornton achieved success in both league and cup competitions.

The first hundred years or this village institution are recorded in a History of the Club published at the time of its centenary in 1980 – copies of which. are available in Menston and other local libraries. The club has had its ups and downs, but has survived two World Wars and enjoyed a continuity rarely achieved by other local sporting and leisure societies.

Bill Bowes on his return from WWII in 1945
(photo by courtesy of The Yorkshire Post).

Notable seasons recorded were 1945, when Bill Bowes of Yorkshire and England turned out to play for the club; 1950, when the first eleven won the Senior League championship and 1951 – the Waddilove Cup.

The Centenary was celebrated with matches played against the more famous M.C.C. and a representative Yorkshire County Side.

Since 1980 the club has achieved success in both League and Cup competitions at Senior and Junior levels.

Something of a 'stir' was created in the League in 1985 when Martin Crowe and Derek Stirling, two New Zealand Test stars, joined the club mid-way through the season to rescue the first XI from possible relegation.

I regard some of Martin Crowe's performances as the finest exhibition of batting and fielding ever likely to be seen in local cricket.

Kenneth Hanson, a popular and generous President for sixteen years, resigned from office in 1985.

Cricket at the Fox and Hounds ground probably between the wars and before the building of Brooklands Park in the 1960's.

An enthusiastic group of junior cricketers in 1970 – several of whom went on to play senior cricket for Menston.

He was succeeded by Ron Beer whose valuable term was highlighted by the erection of a new score-box to the memory of Stanley Atkinson, a Life Member who died in 1988.

David Thackeray was elected President in 1991 and continued in that role until 2010. When he was appointed, it crowned a long distinguished playing career with Menston, spanning nearly forty years. During this time he took over 1400 wickets and scored nearly 8000 runs.

The club continues to make a valuable contribution to the village community and to local cricket, with two senior and three junior teams playing in League and Cup Competitions.

The club's list of members in 1937 – an indication of the measure of support given by the village at this time.

The photograph was taken in April, 1945 when Bill Bowes, the famous Yorkshire and England fast bowler returned from a Prisoner of War Camp in Italy to his home in Bleach Mill Lane, Menston.

The three gentlemen E. Hanson, E. Walker and I. F. Harvey are extending a 'welcome home' to Bill and inviting him to turn out for the Menston village club. This he did – on Whit. Monday, attracting a large crowd, he took 7 wickets for 17 runs against North Leeds.

Throughout the season, without really stretching himself, Bill regularly took five, six and even seven wickets and delighted cricket lovers who came to see him. He bowled 210 overs and took 72 wickets for 8 runs each.

He returned to assist the County in 1946 and his distinguished cricketing career ended in 1947.

In his retirement he became a familiar figure accompanied by his little dog, walking round the village and always ready for a chat.

Many fitting tributes to his memory came from home and abroad when he died, aged seventy-nine, in 1987.

Airedale junior league champions 1946. **Left to right** – ***Back row:*** J. H. Kell, T. Clayton, B. Walker, N. Wormald, H. Hird, A. McKinley, G. Kell. ***Seated:*** A. Simpson, A. Thornton, E. Sutton, B. Bolton (captain), B. Nettleton, A. Maud, I. Town. ***Front row:*** R. Hannam, G. Walker.

Airedale & Wharfedale senior league championship winners 1950. **Left to right** – ***Standing:*** Maurice Warburton, Jack Kell, Cyril Jordan, Harold Metcalfe, Stanley Atkinson, Jack Thornton, Frank Richmond, Jack Morris, Kenneth Barker. **Seated:** Syd Walker, Kenneth Hanson, Eric Thornton (Captain), W. M. Foster-Shepherd (President), Ted Emmerson, Tony Thornton, Brian Nettleton.

Menston Birtwhistle cup winners 1955. **Left to right** – ***Standing:*** D. Bagshaw, G. Hird, E. Wrighton, R. Bowland, M. Ryley, B. Parker, D. E. Thackeray. ***Seated:*** B. Whitehead, M. Lockwood, J. Thornton (Captain), F. Brooking, G. Walker. K. Smith (Scorer).

Five first XI captains. **Left to right:** Paul Smith (1976-77), David Thackeray (1978-80, 1985-86), Ian Town (1960-64), Kenneth Hanson (1956-59), Eric Thornton (1949-52).

Centenary celebration committee 1980. **Left to right** – ***Standing***: Stanley Atkinson, Jack Sullivan, Paul Giles, David Thackeray, Milton Hudson. ***Seated:*** Mike Hughes, Pat Beer, Kenneth Hanson, Dorothy Petch, Jack Kell.

Waddilove cup winners 1983 (V Skipton). **Left to right** – ***Standing:*** Patrick Sullivan, Michael Pratt, Hedley Chapman, David Robinson, John White, Craig Chaplin, Ian Colquhoun, David Lester. ***Seated:*** Simon Richmond, Ron Beer, David Thackeray, Paul Smith, David Manville.

Junior league (West division) champions 1980. **Left to right –** ***Standing:*** Ian Colquhoun, Richard Simpson, Ian Nerurkar, Mark Hornsey, Chris Dewhirst, John Robinson, John Harvey. ***Front row:*** Ian Myers, Steve Hill, Richard Nerurkar, David Lester, Robert Templar.

In 1985 – the mid-season signing of two New Zealand test players sent shock waves round the local cricket leagues. **Left to right:** Derek Stirling, David Lester, David Thackeray, Martin Crowe.

MENSTON CRICKET CLUB.

SEASON, 1937.

THE

Annual General Meeting

of this Club will be held

On Monday, February 7th, 1938,

AT THE COUNCIL SCHOOL,
MAIN STREET, MENSTON.

Chair to be taken at 8 p.m. prompt.

The attendance of all Subscribers and Members is specially desired.

Agenda of Meeting :—

Minutes of Last General Meeting
Secretary's Report
Treasurer's Statement of Accounts
Election of Officers
Members' Business

The Annual Dinner will be held on Friday, February 25th, at 7-0 p.m. at the Fox & Hounds, Hotel. Tickets 2/- each.

Dixons (1930) Ltd., Printers, Guiseley and Yeadon.

Notice of a General Meeting 1937.

Receipts and Payments Account

FOR SEASON 1937.

RECEIPTS.

				£	s.	d.
To Balances brought forward—						
Bank	38	16	3			
Cash	3	1	8			
				41	17	11
,, Subscriptions				71	8	0
,, Gate Receipts				10	0	0
,, Teas				10	5	11
,, Letting of Field and Tackle ...				9	0	0
,, Proceeds from Dances				22	4	10
,, Bank Interest				0	3	0
				£164	19	8

PAYMENTS.

				£	s.	d.
By Tackle				11	13	0
,, Ground Expenses				30	18	5
,, Motor Mower Expenses				19	0	9
,, Umpires and Scorers				9	10	9
,, Rent of Field				18	8	0
,, Insurances				3	5	9
,, League Subscriptions				4	3	0
,, Printing, Stationery and Postages ...				5	7	0
,, Gas and Water				0	16	1
,, Travelling Expenses				13	14	0
,, Land Tax				1	1	4
,, Sundries				1	9	1
,, General Repairs				3	12	11
,, Balances carried forward—						
Bank	39	16	7			
Cash	2	3	0			
				41	19	7
				£164	19	8

We hereby Certify that the above accounts are correct in accordance with the books, vouchers, and information supplied.

Dated this the 25th day of January, 1938.

HOLLINGS, CROWE, STORR & CO.,
Incorporated Accountants,
Hon. Auditors.
Midland Bank Chambers, OTLEY.

W. FLETCHER,
Hon. Treasurer.

Notice of a General Meeting 1937 (continued as opposite).

SUBSCRIPTIONS FOR 1937.

	£	s.	d.
Mr. I. F. Harvey	5	5	0
Mrs. Waddilove	5	0	0
Mr. L. Greaves	2	10	0
Mr. C. Breare	2	2	0
British Legion	2	2	0
Mr. S. Harland	2	0	0
Mr. J. A. Bacon	1	1	0
Mr. C. Butterfield	1	1	0
Mr. N. H. Farrar	1	1	0
Dr. Hyslop	1	1	0
Mr. Pollard	1	1	0
Mr. F. G. Porritt	1	1	0
Mr. H. Sharp	1	1	0
Mr. A. Shaw	1	1	0
Mr. C. M. Tankard	1	1	0
Mr. R. Whitaker	1	1	0
Mr. J. O. Seager	1	0	0
Mr. F. Wigglesworth	1	0	0
Mr. J. W. Willis	1	0	0
Mr. Bateman	0	10	6
Mr. L. Bell	0	10	6
Mr. L. Booth	0	10	6
Mr. B. Breare	0	10	6
Dr. Edgerley	0	10	6
Mr. H. A. Gill	0	10	6
Mr. H. Hargrave	0	10	6
Mr. J. A. Hird	0	10	6
Mr. D. Illingworth	0	10	6
Mr. G. Lawson	0	10	6
Mr. H. Longden	0	10	6
Mr. Newsham	0	10	6
Mr. A. Outtersides	0	10	6
Mr. T. Owston	0	10	6
Mr. W. B. Pickles	0	10	6
Mr. W. E. Raspin	0	10	6
Mr. S. Ryley	0	10	6
Mr. T. H. Toothill	0	10	6
Mr. N. Sowden	0	10	6
Mr. A. Voigt	0	10	6
Mr. G. C. Walter	0	10	6
Mr. S. Waterhouse	0	10	6
Mr. A. Young	0	10	6
Mr. E. Barratt	0	10	0
Mr. S. Biltcliffe	0	10	0
Mr. C. B. Cribb	0	10	0
Mr. R. T. Foulger	0	10	0
Mr. L. A. Gill	0	10	0
Mr. E. Hanson	0	10	0
Mr. C. A. Hardy	0	10	0
Rev. Hodd	0	10	0
Mr. E. K. Ives	0	10	0
Mr. H. B. Kelly	0	10	0
Dr. T. Rankine	0	10	0
Mr. G. Rimmington	0	10	0
Mr. C. W. Smith	0	10	0
Mr. F. Wall	0	10	0
Mr. G. Butler	0	7	6
Dr. R. J. Gourlay	0	7	6
Mr. F. Hall	0	7	6
Mr. H. Hurcombe	0	7	6
Mr. E. Walker	0	7	6
Mr. M. Appleby	0	5	0
Mr. S. Atkinson	0	5	0
Mr. Beaumont	0	5	0
Mr. Bentley	0	5	0
Mr. G. Blackburn	0	5	0
Mr. R. W. Boocock	0	5	0
Mr. Roland Brown	0	5	0
Mr. J. Brennan	0	5	0
Mr. H. Butler	0	5	0
Mr. T. J. Colley	0	5	0
Mr. J. E. Dalton	0	5	0
Mr. A. C. Demaine	0	5	0
Mr. K. Gibson	0	5	0
Mr. A. Hannam	0	5	0
Mr. H. Hannam	0	5	0

	£	s.	d.
Mr. G. Holden	0	5	0
Mr. F. Holland	0	5	0
Mr. W. Johnson	0	5	0
Mr. W. Jones	0	5	0
Mr. G. Kell	0	5	0
Mrs. R. Kell	0	5	0
Mr. E. Kirwan	0	5	0
Mr. N. Lacy	0	5	0
Mr. A. Leach	0	5	0
Mr. W. B. Lee	0	5	0
Mr. J. A. Long	0	5	0
Mr. E. Maloney	0	5	0
Mr. Marchmont	0	5	0
Mr. A. Maston	0	5	0
Mr. J. S. Matthews	0	5	0
Mr. H. K. Morse	0	5	0
Mr. S. Morse	0	5	0
Mrs. Mularky	0	5	0
Mr. J. Newton	0	5	0
Mr. A. Nicholson	0	5	0
Mr. F. Ramsden	0	5	0
Mr. F. Redman	0	5	0
Mr. F. Richmond	0	5	0
Mr. H. Rhodes	0	5	0
Mr. G. Robertshaw	0	5	0
Mr. W. Speak	0	5	0
Mr. W. E. Storr	0	5	0
Mr. F. Dumville	0	5	0
Mr. J. Sutton	0	5	0
Mr. F. Thorpe	0	5	0
Mr. J. Turner	0	5	0
Mr. Upton	0	5	0
Mr. J. H. Vickers	0	5	0
Mr. G. Waite	0	5	0
Mr. J. Walker	0	5	0
Mr. E. Willis	0	5	0
Mr. A. Wilson	0	5	0
Mr. Wilson	0	5	0
Mr. A. Weightman	0	5	0
Mr. R. Weightman	0	5	0
Mr. J. P. Whitfield	0	5	0
Mr. F. Aveyard	0	2	6
Mr. J. Boyes	0	2	6
Mr. F. Brooking	0	2	6
Mr. C. Brown	0	2	6
Mr. J. Clapham	0	2	6
Mr. P. Frazell	0	2	6
Mr. P. Gill	0	2	6
Mr. — Goddard	0	2	6
Mr. D. Hancock	0	2	6
Mr. J. Hanson	0	2	6
Mr. K. Hanson	0	2	6
Mr. H. Hargrave	0	2	6
Mr. E. Holdsworth	0	2	6
Mr. J. Heaton	0	2	6
Mr. K. Jackson	0	2	6
Mr. C. Jordan	0	2	6
Mr. J. Kell	0	2	6
Mr. D. Kyte	0	2	6
Mr. K. Maston	0	2	6
Mr. H. Metcalfe	0	2	6
Mr. W. Murray	0	2	6
Mr. Alan Peel	0	2	6
Mr. W. Peel	0	2	6
Mr. D. Pollard	0	2	6
Mr. K. Norman	0	2	6
Mr. D. Outtersides	0	2	6
Mr. C. Outtersides	0	2	6
Mr. J. Robertshaw	0	2	6
Mr. T. Robertshaw	0	2	6
Mr. P. Robinson	0	2	6
Mr. P. Smirthwaite	0	2	6
Mr. W. Wright	0	2	6
	£71	8	0

Life Members :—

Mr. W. Fletcher, Mr. J. W. Willis.

SOME VILLAGE PERSONALITIES

Margaret Harvey at the Bramham Moor Hunter Trials 1958 (*Yorkshire Post*).

Margaret Harvey

The village would not be the same without Horses and Riders. In my youth, there were horses to hire at Walker's Springbank Stables down Menston Old Lane and more recently, stables have been established at the Home Farm off Bingley Road.

For nearly 50 years, however, village equestrian activity has been dominated by Margaret Harvey.

The Wharfedale Riding School and the Yorkshire Dales Trekking Centre were established by her in the early fifties. (She was a pioneer in pony trekking in England).

In over 40 years Margaret has been involved in breeding and training horses and ponies to reach the highest standard in local and national show jumping.

Hundreds of young riders have been trained by her – many to become champions. Others have benefited from her experience to start, and run, their own riding establishments.

Perhaps her most famous horse was Wharfedale Kestrel which she bred and qualified to jump in the Horse of the Year Show Final.

Margaret has served on the Wharfedale Agricultural Show Horse Committee for 40 years, supplied horses for film work, trained teams for Duke of Edinburgh gold and silver awards and the long list of her awards and champions, too numerous to mention, indicate she has simply lived horses!

Elsie Fletcher FRSA

Miss Elsie Fletcher FRSA.

Menston's indefatigable historian published numerous booklets of local interest.

Her main works concerning the village were *The Menston Story* published in 1953 and *Menston Hall – its Manor and Site 971-1971*.

Miss Fletcher (she died aged 88 in 1974) was the first curator of the Ilkley Manor House Museum and was particularly interested in the Roman Occupation of the West Riding.

In 1910 she founded a private Kindergarten and Junior School at her home 'Howdene' in Bradford Road, Menston.

Miss Fletcher's father, Walter, was a life member of Menston Cricket Club. His ashes were spread on the cricket field, as were those of Edward Hanson and Stanley Atkinson.

Beatrice Porritt

Beatrice Porritt with her 1936 MGPB. *(Photo by Auto Express).*

Until overtaken by a debilitating illness, Miss Porritt was a familiar figure in village and local circles. She died in 1997.

She was born in Bradford, spent her early years in Australia and, since the early thirties, a generous supporter of most village organisations.

Her car was her 'friend' for many years, was a 1936 supercharged MGPB.

Miss Porritt was the owner of the field in Cleasby Road – one of the few possible remaining building areas in the village.

Largely due to the strenuous efforts of Mrs Audrey Brand, former Chairman of Ilkley Parish Council, the field has now been adopted by the Burley, Menston Charities Trust and, in accordance with Miss Porritt's wishes, will be 'kept an open space in perpetuity in memory of her parents'.

A substantial sum of money has also been allocated by Miss Porritt for the upkeep of the field.

Jimmy Bolton – a familiar road sweeper in the village for many years. A presentation, launched by Dr. Shaw and subscribed to by residents, marked his retirement in 1965.

Jimmy Bolton.

October 1982. New vicar of Menston Rev. Irvin Wilson meets some of his parishioners – including Dr. David Purdie. Both Rev. Wilson and Dr. Purdie died during 1987. (Copyright courtesy of *Wharfedale Observer*)

Richard Nerurkar

The famous International runner spent much of his early life in Menston where his parents lived.

Richard attended the Junior School and was captain of a successful Menston Junior Cricket team.

He was an enthusiastic member of the Scout movement and his athleticism helped the Menston Guy troop to win the Annual Chevin Torch Relay Race on numerous occasions.

During his period with the Scouts he and his brother Ian were members of the party to represent Wharfedale at the 1978 World Jamboree in the USA.

Richard Nerurkar MBE

His distinguished athletic career was launched at Bradford Grammar School, where he won the Northern Schools title.

Progressing to Oxford University, Richard gained an athletic blue. Joining Bingley Harriers he achieved national success in Cross Country Championships and was English Champion in 1990, 1991 and 1993.

Other major achievements:

Winner of the AAA 10,000m in 1990. Represented Great Britain in World Championships in 1991 and 1995. The Olympic Games in 1992 and European Championships in 1990 and 1994.

In 1993 he came first in the Marathon in Hamburg and, later in the same year, won the World Cup (Marathon) in San Sebastian. In 1995, in Seoul, he was second and seventh in the World Championship Marathon in Sweden.

Richard's academic achievements equal his running and this modest young man holds degrees in Russian and German (University College, Oxford) and in Public Administration from Harvard University in the USA.

He was awarded the MBE in 2003 for his organisation of the Great Ethiopian Run involving 15,000 competitors in the African continent.

Nigel Melville

The former England Rugby Union Captain lived, with his parents, in Cleasby Road before his marriage to Miss Susan Waddington in 1987 (Internationals Rob Andrews and Rory Underwood were guests).

Nigel began his rugby at Aireborough Grammar School and with Otley R.U.F.C. He won County and International caps as a schoolboy and colt.

In 1983 he was selected to play for England against Scotland but had to withdraw because of injury. He toured New Zealand with the British Lions and was appointed Captain of England – on his debut – against Australia in 1984.

Nigel played a dozen internationals for England with distinction, but various injuries curtailed his brilliant career and he retired from the game – for the 3rd time – in 1995.

In 1988 he took up coaching and began with his local club, Otley. The game became professional in 1996 and Nigel was director of rugby for Wasps and then Gloucester before being appointed chief executive officer and president of rugby operations for United States Rugby in 2006.

Nigel Melville in his playing days.

Eric Knight creator of *Lassie come home*

A famous Menston personality, only recently recognised was Eric Knight the author of *Lassie come home*.

He was born at Carlrayne Villa, Menston in 1897. When 2 years old Knight's father deserted the family, went to South Africa and was killed in the Boar War. His mother re married and eventually emigrated to the U.S.A.

Eric stayed in Yorkshire until he was 15 years old and then followed his mother to America. He became involved with newspaper and film work.

An early ambition to write a novel resulted in the best seller 'Lassie come home'. The book became world famous, was published in 25 languages and is regarded as a classic.

The movie featuring Lassie was released in 1943 but Eric did not live long enough to see the legend he created.

On the 15th of January 1943 he was killed in action on a Douglas transport plane which crashed on its way to Casablanca. He was 45 years old and one of 35 killed.

Writer Greg Christie has thoroughly researched the life of this remarkable, history making man who came from Menston.

Smith Wigglesworth

Smith Wigglesworth, the famous evangelist, was born in Menston in 1859. His parents John and Martha were both weavers and lived in a row of cottages, now demolished at the foot of Derry Hill (shown page 167).

Smith started work at 6 years old doing farm work. As a boy his grandmother, Bella, took him to the first Menston chapel which still exists and now used as an artists studio. He could neither read or write on leaving school but learnt the trade of a plumber. When he was 13 the family moved to Bradford and, when 20, it is recorded he went to Liverpool.

His deep Christian faith led him to America where his evangelism took him to the fame he experienced for many years.

Several Americans have visited Menston – searching for the birthplace of Smith Wigglesworth.

Some Menston Artists

In addition to those previously recorded – Francis Wall, John Cooper and Florence Anderson, I must include artists Ian Town and Mark Thompson. They have both extended their artistry to the restoration of buildings.

Ian, a commercial artist learnt his trade in Bradford and firmly established himself before emigrating, with his wife and family to New Zealand 40 years ago. He was an outstanding cricketer – for Menston and in the Bradford League. His painting *Cricket at The Fox* shows his artistic ability and I feel indicates his love of Menston which he has never lost.

Cricket at The Fox by Ian Town.

Mark has an exceptional natural ability in the art world. As a teenager he cycled all over Yorkshire with his sketch pad and started to sell his drawings. He rented a Tudor house at Barden Tower from the Duchess of Devonshire and later managed a tea room at Middleham. For several years he kept the Kings Arms in Reeth and is now landlord of the Green Dragon near Hawes, behind which is Hardraw Force and the renowned bandstand. Mark is still producing splendid artwork and restoring old buildings. A few years ago he bought Nappa Hall, a 15th century manor house in Wensleydale.

Well House by Mark Thompson.

Queens Golden Jubilee 2002

Marking the Queens golden jubilee, in 2002, councilor Richard Wightman, Lord Mayor of Bradford, living in Fairfax Hall, plants a golden ash tree at the corner of Main Street and Stocks Hill – hundreds of villagers turned out to watch him.

There are a number of groups, activities and events in this village of ours that deserve more commendation and space than this treatise can give, including the skateboard park, Gardeners Club, Menston Cares, the move of Abbeyfield from Cleasby Road to the Beeches and Menston in Bloom with Founder David Nerukar. No doubt they will follow in a later history of Menston.

The closing of Highroyds Hospital and, in Buckle Lane, the promotion of a new group – Friends of Highroyds Memorial Garden, which has restored the cemetary containing over 2000, former patients in unmarked graves. The group is now restoring the chapel.

Increasing concern for the green belt and formation of a busy, vital group – Menston Action Group, opposing a decision by Bradford Council to build 600 houses in the areas of Derry Hill and Bingley Road.

In 2012 Councillor Dale Smith was elected Lord Mayor of Bradford. Margaret his wife became Lady Mayoress.

Richard Wightman, Lord Mayor of Bradford planting a tree marking the Queen's Golden Jubilee.